THE
ADVENTURES OF BUFFALO BILL

HE SAW THE FEATHERED HEAD OF AN INDIAN POKE OVER
THE BANK BEFORE HIM.

The Adventures of Buffalo Bill

BY
COL. WILLIAM F. CODY
(BUFFALO BILL)

The Naval & Military Press Ltd

Published by

The Naval & Military Press Ltd

Unit 5 Riverside, Brambleside
Bellbrook Industrial Estate
Uckfield, East Sussex
TN22 1QQ England

Tel: +44 (0)1825 749494

www.naval-military-press.com
www.nmarchive.com

CONTENTS

THE ADVENTURES OF BUFFALO BILL

THE LIFE OF BUFFALO BILL

ILLUSTRATIONS

FOREWORD

WITH the death of William Frederick Cody, at Denver on January 10, 1917, there passed away the last of that intrepid band of pathfinders who gave their lives to the taming of the West, a gallant company of brave men steadfastly pushing back the frontier year by year and mile by mile, and ceasing from their labors only when the young and vigorous life of the Pacific States had been linked up for all time with the older civilization of the Atlantic seaboard.

The fame of Colonel Cody, or Buffalo Bill as he was popularly called, recalls that of Daniel Boone, Davy Crockett, and Kit Carson, but he cannot be said to rank with those earlier heroes in point of actual national service. He played no large part in the upbuilding of our Continental Empire. Yet he was made of the same stern stuff, and, on his more circumscribed stage, he was a gallant and picturesque figure, a true super-

FOREWORD

man of the brave old days. When, in 1883,
Cody gave up his roving life and organized
the Wild West show it meant that the Wild
West itself was gone for good and all. Together with Boone, Crockett, and Carson
his life rounds out the century of continental
occupation, counting from the year Boone
crossed the mountains into Kentucky to the
final completion of the Union Pacific Railway. Boone was born in Pennsylvania and
died in Missouri; Crockett was born west
of the Alleghanies, in Tennessee, and died
in Texas; Carson and Cody were born west
of the Mississippi, and died in Colorado.

Perhaps the most picturesque period in
Buffalo Bill's life was his service as a rider
in the service of the famous Pony Express
just before the Civil War. This was perhaps the most perilous job that a man could
undertake, and young Cody was barely
fifteen years old. Yet he had had previous
experience in Indian fighting and at the age
of eleven he had killed his first Indian.
Shortly afterward the Civil War began and
Cody enlisted in the Union Army, serving
as a scout. When the fighting was over he

returned to the Far West. The transcontinental railways were in process of construction, a romantic episode in American history fittingly depicted in the glowing pages of Zane Grey's *The U. P. Trail.* The builders of the Kansas Pacific Railroad wanted buffalo meat to feed their laborers and Cody undertook the contract. In eighteen months (1867-68) he killed 4,280 buffaloes, and thereby earned his title of Buffalo Bill.

In 1868 Cody rejoined the army as scout and guide, and quickly made a reputation as a man of infinite endurance and daring. He was attached to General Sheridan's headquarters at Hays City, Kansas; and soon after reporting for duty he learned that the commander wanted a dispatch sent to Fort Dodge, a distance of ninety-five miles. The Indians had recently killed two or three dispatch riders on this route, and none of the scouts was anxious to take on the job. Even a promised bonus of several hundred dollars found no takers. Cody volunteered and made the dangerous trip in safety. But at Fort Dodge he found that the commanding officer there was very anxious to send dispatches to Fort Larned, and again the regular scouts shunned the task. On went Buffalo Bill to Fort Larned, sixty-five miles farther. About half-way he stopped to water his mule and the animal got away from him. For thirty-five miles Cody trailed the obstinate brute on foot, never quite able to get within clutch of his bridle rein. At daybreak Fort Larned came in sight and the danger from roving Indians was over. "Now, Mr. Mule, it is my turn," exclaimed the exhausted and thoroughly infuriated scout, raising his gun to his shoulder. Like the majority of Government mules he was not easy to kill. He died hard, but he died.

After a few hours' sleep it was necessary to begin the return journey, as answering dispatches had to be sent to General Sheridan. Again the ride was made in safety, and one of the greatest feats in all scout history had been accomplished. It should be explained that, previous to beginning the ride to Fort Dodge, Cody had been in the saddle for twenty hours, covering a distance of 140 miles. His grand total for a period of fifty-

eight hours was 365 miles (including thirty-
five miles on foot), an average of over six
miles an hour.

A little later Cody was appointed chief
scout and guide for the Fifth Cavalry in a
campaign against the hostile Sioux and
Cheyennes, and he had many narrow escapes
from the tight places into which his adven-
turous disposition was always leading him.
He also served as chief scout for the Republican River Expedition of 1869.

While living near Fort McPherson, Nebraska, in 1870, Cody was appointed justice
of the peace by General Emory to take care
of certain civilian offenders against the common law. Buffalo Bill protested that he
knew nothing about law, but General
Emory was insistent and Cody went over to
North Platte and was sworn in. That very
night he was aroused by a man who had a
complaint to make. One of his horses had
been stolen by the boss of a passing herd,
and he wanted a writ of replevin. "I don't
know what a replevin is," answered 'Squire
Cody, as he took down his old Lucretia rifle
and patted it gently, "but I guess this will

do as well." In company with the com-
plainant Cody galloped after the cavalcade
and soon overtook the offender against the
ethical code. At first the boss was defiant,
but when he realized who the 'Squire was
he quickly weakened. "I didn't care a blank
about you being justice of the peace and con-
stable combined," he explained, "but when
I found out you were Buffalo Bill it was
time to lay down my hand." The 'Squire
read the fellow a lecture on the iniquity
of horse stealing, collected a fine of one
hundred and fifty dollars, reclaimed the
animal, and declared that court was ad-
journed.

In 1872 the Russian Grand Duke Alexis
visited this country, and a Far West hunting expedition was arranged in his honor.
Buffalo Bill acted as guide and chief hunts-
man. The Grand Duke, under Cody's
tutelage, succeeded in bagging several hand-
some heads, and, in token of his apprecia-
tion, he presented to Buffalo Bill his almost
priceless fur overcoat and a wonderful set
of sleeve links and scarfpin studded with
diamonds and rubies. In this same year

FOREWORD

Cody was elected a member of the Nebraska Legislature. Later on he resigned and went to Chicago, where he made his first appearance on the stage as an actor in a play written around himself and entitled, "The Scout of the Plains."

In 1874 Cody acted as guide to a grand hunting party given by General Sheridan to a number of wealthy and distinguished Eastern men. Cody became a great favorite with everybody, and the next winter he went on to New York to visit his new friends. He wore his famous sombrero and his fringed hunting suit of buckskin everywhere, and they created a mild sensation on Broadway and Fifth Avenue. Then he went back to the West and tried the humdrum life of a farmer and ranchman.

The famous Wild West show was staged for the first time at Omaha on May 17, 1883. It was a tremendous success from the start, and Colonel Cody was besieged with applications from all over the country. He went to England in 1887; royalty patronized this truly original and thrilling entertainment, and Buffalo Bill's fortune was

made. In later years several successful
European tours were undertaken.

In November, 1911, Colonel Cody announced his retirement. He was then sixty-
seven years old and reputed to be worth
$3,000,000. He went to his ranch at Cody,
Wyoming, and tried to settle down. But
the old spirit of adventure lured him back
to the sawdust arena. This time he was not
so fortunate. He lost money on every hand,
and finally the celebrated show went under
the auctioneer's hammer. Friends came to
his rescue, however, and bid in his famous
white horse, Ishan, which the Colonel always rode at the head of his roughriders.

The old scout had kept his courage, too,
and he announced his intention of trying it
again; he even joined a circus company as
one of the regular troupe of performers.
But his race was run, his day was done.
Even his iron constitution had been weakened by the trials and privations of seventy-
two years of strenuous life. He had lived
up to the very last inch of his allotted span.
He had played hard and he had fought hard
and in the end he died hard, amazing even

his experienced physicians by his extraordinary vitality. The doctors had told him that the end was near, but he only laughed and called for a pack of cards. "You can't kill the old scout," he said, smilingly. "Let's have a game of high-five." Yet even this undaunted spirit was forced to bow to mortal necessity, and a day or two later he relapsed into a state of unconsciousness from which he was never to emerge.

His death attracted the notice of two continents. The newspapers printed columns of obituaries; the State of Colorado ordered a public funeral in his honor; it was the passing of a heroic figure in American annals. All in all, he must rank as the greatest of scouts and the most gallant of Indian fighters. He never knew fear. His life was in danger hundreds of times, and yet he always had the better of his adversary. He lived a free life among wild surroundings, but he was always to be found on the side of law and order. He was a dead shot, a splendid horseman, and an absolutely fearless fighter. The men who knew him best, including many well-known

FOREWORD

officers of the army, all united in praising the bravery, honesty, and modesty of this true product of the old wild West. His place can never be filled; he was a relic of the days that are gone, never to return.

THE ADVENTURES OF
BUFFALO BILL

THE ADVENTURES OF
BUFFALO BILL

I

CROSSING THE PLAINS

IN the early settlement of Kansas common-school advantages were denied us, and to provide a means for educating the few boys and girls in the neighborhood of my home, a subscription school was started in a small log cabin that was built on the bank of a creek that ran near our house. My mother took great interest in this school, and at her persuasion I returned home and became enrolled as a pupil, where I made satisfactory progress until, as the result of a quarrel with a schoolmate, I left the town and started across the plains with one of Russell, Majors & Waddell's freight trains.

The trip proved a most enjoyable one to me, although no incidents worthy of note occurred on the way. On my return from

Fort Kearny I was paid off the same as the rest of the employés. The remainder of the summer and fall I spent in herding cattle and working for Russell, Majors & Waddell.

In May, 1857, I started for Salt Lake City with a herd of beef cattle, in charge of Frank and Bill McCarthy, for General Albert Sidney Johnston's army, which was then being sent across the plains to fight the Mormons.

Nothing occurred to interrupt our journey until we reached Plum Creek, on the South Platte River, thirty-five miles west of old Fort Kearny. We had made a morning drive, and had camped for dinner. The wagon masters and a majority of the men had gone to sleep under the mess wagons. The cattle were being guarded by three men, and the cook was preparing dinner. No one had any idea that Indians were anywhere near us. The first warning we had that they were infesting that part of the country was the firing of shots and the whoops and yells from a party of them, who, catching us napping, gave us a most unwelcome surprise. All the men jumped to their feet and seized their guns. They saw with astonishment the cattle running in every direction, they having been stampeded by the Indians, who had shot and killed the three men who were on day herd duty, and the redmen were now charging down upon the rest of us.

The McCarthy boys, at the proper moment, gave orders to fire upon the advancing enemy. The volley checked them, although they returned the compliment, and shot one of our party through the leg. Frank McCarthy then sang out, "Boys, make a break for the slough yonder, and we can then have the bank for a breastwork."

We made a run for the slough, which was only a short distance off, and succeeded in safely reaching it, bringing with us the wounded man. The bank proved to be a very effective breastwork, affording us good protection. We had been there but a short time when Frank McCarthy, seeing that the longer we were corralled the worse it would be for us, said,

"Well, boys, we'll try to make our way

back to Fort Kearny by wading in the river and keeping the bank for a breastwork."

We all agreed that this was the best plan, and we accordingly proceeded down the river several miles in this way, managing to keep the Indians at a safe distance with our guns, until the slough made a junction with the main Platte River. From there down we found the river at times quite deep, and in order to carry the wounded man along with us, we constructed a raft of poles for his accommodation, and in this way he was transported.

Occasionally the water would be too deep for us to wade, and we were obliged to put our weapons on the raft and swim. The Indians followed us pretty closely, and were continually watching for an opportunity to get a good range and give us a raking fire. Covering ourselves by keeping well under the bank, we pushed ahead as rapidly as possible, and made pretty good progress, the night finding us still on the way and our enemies yet on our track.

I, being the youngest and smallest of the party, became somewhat tired, and, without

4

noticing it, I had fallen behind the others for some little distance. It was about ten o'clock, and we were keeping very quiet and hugging close to the bank, when I happened to look up to the moonlit sky and saw the plumed head of an Indian peeping over the bank. Instead of hurrying ahead and alarming the men in a quiet way, I instantly aimed my gun at his head and fired. The report rang out sharp and loud on the night air, and was immediately followed by an Indian whoop, and the next moment about six feet of dead Indian came tumbling into the river. I was not only overcome with astonishment, but was badly scared, as I could hardly realize what I had done. I expected to see the whole force of Indians come down upon us. While I was standing thus bewildered, the men, who had heard the shot and the war whoop, and had seen the Indian take a tumble, came rushing back.

"Who fired that shot?" cried Frank McCarthy.

"I did," replied I, rather proudly, as my confidence returned, and I saw the men coming up.

"Yes, and little Billy has killed an Indian stone dead—too dead to skin," said one of the men, who had approached nearer than the rest, and had almost stumbled upon the Indian. From that time forward I became a hero and an Indian-killer. This was, of course, the first Indian I had ever shot, and as I was not then more than eleven years of age, my exploit created quite a sensation.

The other Indians, upon learning what had happened to their advance, fired several shots without effect, but which hastened our retreat down the river. We reached Fort Kearny just as the reveille was being sounded, bringing the wounded man with us. After the peril through which we had passed, it was a relief to feel that once more I was safe after such a dangerous initiation.

Frank McCarthy immediately reported to the commanding officer and informed him of all that had happened. The commandant at once ordered a company of cavalry and one of infantry to proceed to Plum Creek on a forced march, taking a howitzer with them—to endeavor to recapture the cattle from the Indians.

CROSSING THE PLAINS

The firm of Russell, Majors & Waddell had a division agent at Kearny, and this agent mounted us on mules so that we could accompany the troops. On reaching the place where the Indians had surprised us, we found the bodies of the three men, whom they had killed and scalped and literally cut into pieces. We of course buried the remains. We caught but few of the cattle, most of them having been driven off and stampeded with the buffaloes, there being numerous immense herds of the latter in that section of the country at the time. The Indians' trail was discovered running south toward the Republican River, and the troops followed it to the head of Plum Creek, and there abandoned it, returning to Fort Kearny without having seen a single redskin.

The company's agent, seeing that there was no further use for us in that vicinity— as we had lost our cattle and mules—sent us back to Fort Leavenworth. The company, it is proper to state, did not have to stand the loss of the expedition, as the government held itself responsible for such depredations by the Indians.

On the day that I got into Leavenworth, some time in July, I was interviewed for the first time in my life by a newspaper reporter, and the next morning I found my name in print as "the youngest Indian-slayer on the plains." I am candid enough to admit that I felt very much elated over this notoriety. Again and again I read with eager interest the long and sensational account of our adventure. My exploit was related in a very graphic manner, and for a long time afterward I was considerable of a hero.

In the following summer, Russell, Majors & Waddell entered upon a contract with the government for General Albert Sidney Johnston's army that was sent against the Mormons. A large number of teams and teamsters were required for the purpose, and as the route was considered a dangerous one, men were not easily engaged for the service, though the pay was forty dollars a month in gold. An old wagon master named Lew Simpson, one of the best that ever commanded a bull train, was upon the point of starting with about ten wagons for the company, direct for Salt Lake, and as he had

8

known me for some time as an ambitious youth, requested me to accompany him as an extra hand. My duties would be light, and, in fact, I would have nothing to do, unless some one of the drivers became sick, in which case I would be required to take his place. But even more seductive than this inducement was the promise that I should be provided with a mule of my own to ride, and be subject to the orders of no one save Simpson himself.

As a matter of interest to the general reader, it may be well to give a brief description of a freight train. The wagons used in those days by Russell, Majors & Waddell were known as the "J. Murphy wagons," made at St. Louis especially for the plains business. They were very large and very strongly built, being capable of carrying seven thousand pounds of freight each. The wagon boxes were very commodious, being about as large as the rooms of an ordinary house, and were covered with two heavy canvas sheets to protect the merchandise from the rain. These wagons were generally sent out from Leavenworth, each loaded with six thousand pounds of freight, and each drawn by several yoke of oxen in charge of one driver. A train consisted of twenty-five wagons, all in charge of one man, who was known as the wagon master. The second man in command was the assistant wagon master. Then came the "extra hand," next the night herder, and lastly the cavayard driver, whose duty it was to drive the loose and lame cattle. There were thirty-one men all told in a train. The men did their own cooking, being divided into messes of seven. One man cooked, another brought wood and water, another stood guard, and so on, each having some duty to perform while getting meals. All were heavily armed with Colt's pistols and Mississippi yagers, and every one always had his weapons handy so as to be prepared for any emergency.

The wagon master, in the language of the plains, was called the "bull-wagon boss"; the teamsters were known as "bull-whackers"; and the whole train was denominated a "bull outfit." Everything at that time was called an "outfit." The men of the plains were always full of a droll humor and exciting stories of their own experiences, and many an hour I spent in listening to the recitals of thrilling adventures and hairbreadth escapes.

The trail to Salt Lake ran through Kansas northwestwardly, crossing the Big Blue River, then over the Big and Little Sandy, coming into Nebraska near the Big Sandy. The next stream of any importance was the Little Blue, along which the trail ran for sixty miles, then crossed a range of sand hills, and struck the Platte River ten miles below Fort Kearny; thence the course lay up the South Platte to the old Ash Hollow Crossing; thence eighteen miles across to the North Platte, near the mouth of the Blue Water, where General Harney had his great battle in 1855 with the Sioux and Cheyenne Indians. From this point the North Platte was followed, passing Courthouse Rock, Chimney Rock, and Scott's Bluffs, and then on to Fort Laramie, where the Laramie River was crossed. Still following the North Platte for some considerable distance, the trail crossed the river at old Richard's

Bridge, and followed it up to the celebrated Red Buttes, crossing the Willow Creeks to the Sweet Water, thence past the Cold Springs, where, three feet under the sod, on the hottest day of summer, ice can be found; thence to the Hot Springs and the Rocky Ridge, and through the Rocky Mountains and Echo Canyon, and thence on to the great Salt Lake Valley.

Nothing occurred on the trip to delay or give us any trouble whatever, until the train struck the South Platte River. One day we camped on the same ground where the Indians had surprised the cattle herd in charge of the McCarthy brothers. It was with difficulty that we discovered any traces of anybody ever having camped there before, the only landmark being the single grave, now covered with grass, in which we had buried the three men who had been killed. The country was alive with buffaloes, and having a day of rare sport, we captured ten or twelve head of cattle, they being a portion of the herd which had been stampeded by the Indians two months before. The next day we pulled out of the camp, and the train was strung out to a considerable length along the road which ran near the foot of the sand hills two miles from the river. Between the road and the river we saw a large herd of buffaloes grazing quietly, they having been down to the stream for a drink.

Just at this time we observed a party of returning Californians coming from the West. They too noticed the buffalo herd, and in another moment they were dashing down upon them, urging their steeds to the greatest speed. The buffalo herd stampeded at once, and broke down the hills. So hotly were they pursued by the hunters that about five hundred of them rushed through our train pell-mell, frightening both men and oxen. Some of the wagons were turned clear around, and many of the terrified oxen attempted to run to the hills, with the heavy wagons attached to them. Others turned around so short that they broke the wagon tongues off. Nearly all the teams got entangled in their gearing, and became wild and unruly, so that the perplexed drivers were unable to manage them.

The buffaloes, the cattle, and the drivers were soon running in every direction, and the excitement upset nearly everybody and everything. Many of the cattle broke their yokes and stampeded. One big buffalo bull became entangled in one of the heavy wagon chains, and it is a fact that in his desperate efforts to free himself he not only actually snapped the strong chain in two, but broke the ox yoke to which it was attached, and the last seen of him he was running toward the hills with it hanging from his horns. A dozen other equally remarkable incidents happened during the short time that the frantic buffaloes were playing havoc with our train, and when they got through and left us our outfit was badly crippled and scattered. This caused us to go into camp and spend a day in replacing the broken tongues and repairing other damages, and gathering up our scattered ox teams.

The next day we rolled out of camp, and proceeded on our way toward the setting sun. Everything ran along smoothly with us from that point until we came within about eighteen miles of Green River, in the Rocky Mountains, where we camped at noon. At this place we had to drive our cattle about a mile and a half to a creek to water them. Simpson, his assistant George Wood, and myself, accompanied by the usual number of guards, drove the cattle over to the creek, and while on our way back to camp we suddenly observed a party of twenty horsemen rapidly approaching us. We were not yet in view of our wagons, as a rise of ground intervened, and therefore we could not signal the trainmen in case of any unexpected danger befalling us. We had no suspicion, however, that we were about to be trapped, as the strangers were white men. When they had come up to us, one of the party, who evidently was the leader, rode out in front, and said,

"How are you, Mr. Simpson?"

"You've got the best of me, sir," said Simpson, who did not know him.

"Well, I rather think I have," coolly replied the stranger, whose words conveyed a double meaning, as we soon learned. We had all come to a halt by this time, and the strange horsemen had surrounded us. They were all armed with double-barreled shotguns, rifles, and revolvers. We also were armed with revolvers, but we had no idea of danger, and these men, much to our surprise, had "got the drop" on us, and had covered us with their weapons, so that we were completely at their mercy. The whole movement of corralling us was done so quietly and quickly that it was accomplished before we knew it.

"I'll trouble you for your six-shooters, gentlemen," now said the leader.

"I'll give 'em to you in a way you don't want," replied Simpson.

The next moment three guns were leveled at Simpson. "If you make a move you are a dead man," said the leader.

Simpson saw at a glance that he was taken at a great disadvantage, and thinking it advisable not to risk the lives of the party by any rash act on his part, he said, "I see now that you have the best of me; but who are you, anyhow?"

"I am Joe Smith," was the reply.

"What! the leader of the Danites?" asked Simpson.

"You are correct," said Smith, for he it was.

"Yes," said Simpson, "I know you now; you are a spying scoundrel."

Simpson had good reason for calling him this, for only a short time before this Joe Smith had visited our train in the disguise of a teamster, and had remained with us two days. He suddenly disappeared, no one knowing where he had gone or why he had come among us. But it was all explained to us, now that he had returned with his Mormon Danites. After they had disarmed us, Simpson asked,

"Well, Smith, what are you going to do with us?"

"Ride back with us and I'll soon show you," said Smith.

We had no idea of the surprise which awaited us. As we came upon the top of the ridge from which we could view our camp, we were astonished to see the remainder of the trainmen disarmed and stationed in a group, and surrounded by another squad of Danites, while other Mormons were searching our wagons for such articles as they wanted.

"How is this?" inquired Simpson. "How did you surprise my camp without a struggle? I can't understand it?"

"Easily enough," said Smith. "Your men were all asleep under the wagons, except the cooks, who saw us coming, and took us for returning Californians or emigrants, and paid no attention to us until we rode up and surrounded your train. With our arms covering the men, we woke them up, and told them all they had to do was to walk out and drop their pistols, which they saw was the best thing they could do under circumstances over which they had no control, and you can just bet they did it."

"And what do you propose to do with us now?" asked Simpson.

"I intend to burn your train," said he. "You are loaded with supplies and ammunition for Sidney Johnston, and as I have no way to convey the stuff to my own people, I'll see that it does not reach the United States troops."

"Are you going to turn us adrift here?" asked Simpson, who was anxious to learn what was to become of himself and his men.

"No; I am hardly as bad as that. I'll give you enough provisions to last you until you can reach Fort Bridger," replied Smith. "And as soon as your cooks can get the stuff out of the wagons you can start."

"On foot?" was the laconic inquiry of Simpson.

"Yes, sir," was the equally short reply.

"Smith, that's too rough on us men. Put yourself in our place, and see how you would like it," said Simpson. "You can well afford to give us at least one wagon and six yokes of oxen to convey us and our clothing and provisions to Fort Bridger. You're a brute if you don't do this."

"Well," said Smith, after consulting a minute or two with some of his company, "I'll do that much for you."

The cattle and the wagon were brought up according to his orders, and the clothing and provisions were loaded on.

"Now you can go," said Smith, after everything had been arranged.

"Joe Smith, I think you are a mean coward to set us afloat in a hostile country without giving us our arms," said Simpson, who had once before asked for the weapons, and had had his request denied.

Smith, after further consultation with his comrades, said: "Simpson, you are too brave a man to be turned adrift here without any means of defense. You shall have your revolvers and guns."

Our weapons were accordingly handed over to Simpson, and we at once started for Fort Bridger, knowing that it would be useless to attempt the recapture of the train.

When we had traveled about two miles we saw the smoke arising from our old camp. The Mormons, after taking what goods they wanted and could carry off, had set fire to the wagons, many of which were loaded with bacon, lard, hardtack, and other provisions, which made a very hot, fierce fire, and the smoke to roll up in dense clouds. Some of the wagons were loaded with ammunition, and it was not long before loud explosions followed in rapid succession. We waited and witnessed the burning of the train, and then pushed on to Fort Bridger. Arriving at this post, we learned that two other trains had been captured and destroyed in the same way by the Mormons. This made seventy-five wagonloads, or four hundred and fifty thousand pounds of supplies, mostly provisions, which never reached General Johnston's command, to which they had been consigned.

After reaching the fort, it being far in November, we decided to spend the winter there, with about four hundred other employés of Russell, Majors & Waddell, rather than attempt a return, which would have exposed us to many dangers and the severity of the rapidly approaching winter. During this period of hibernation, however, the larders of the commissary became so depleted that we were placed on one-quarter rations, and at length, as a final resort, the poor, dreadfully emaciated mules and oxen were killed to afford sustenance for our famishing party.

Fort Bridger being located in a prairie, all fuel there used had to be carried for a distance of nearly two miles, and after our mules and oxen were butchered, we had no other recourse than to carry the wood on our backs or haul it on sleds—a very tedious and laborious alternative.

Starvation was beginning to lurk about the post when spring approached, and but for the timely arrival of a westward-bound train loaded with provisions for Johnston's army, some of our party must certainly have fallen victims to deadly hunger.

The winter finally passed away, and early in the spring, as soon as we could travel, the civil employés of the government, with the teamsters and freighters, started for the Missouri River, the Johnston expedition having been abandoned.

On the way up we stopped at Fort Laramie, and there met a supply train bound westward. Of course we all had a square meal once more, consisting of hardtack, bacon, coffee, and beans. I can honestly say that I thought it was the best meal that I had ever eaten; at least I relished it more than any other, and I think the rest of the party did the same.

On leaving Fort Laramie, Simpson was

made brigadier wagon master, and was put in charge of two large trains, with about four hundred extra men who were bound for Fort Leavenworth. When we came to Ash Hollow, instead of taking the usual trail over to the South Platte, Simpson concluded to follow the North Platte down to its junction with the South Platte. The two trains were traveling about fifteen miles apart, when one morning, while Simpson was with the rear train, he told his assistant wagon master George Wood and myself to saddle up our mules, as he wanted us to go with him and overtake the head train.

We started off at about eleven o'clock, and had ridden about seven miles, when, while we were on a big plateau back of Cedar Bluffs, we suddenly discovered a band of Indians coming out of the head of the ravine half a mile distant, and charging down upon us at full speed. I thought that our end had come this time. Simpson, however, was equal to the occasion, for with wonderful promptness he jumped from his jaded mule, and in a trice shot his own animal and ours also, and ordered us to assist him to jerk their bodies into a triangle. This being quickly done, we got inside the barricade of mule-flesh, and were prepared to receive the Indians. We were each armed with a Mississippi yager and two revolvers, and as the Indians came swooping down on our improvised fort, we opened fire with such good effect that three fell dead at the first volley. This caused them to retreat out of range, as with two exceptions they were armed with bows and arrows, and therefore to approach near enough to do execution would expose at least several of them to certain death. Seeing that they could not take our little fortification or drive us from it, they circled around several times, shooting their arrows at us. One of these struck George Wood in the left shoulder, inflicting only a slight wound, however, and several lodged in the bodies of the dead mules; otherwise they did us no harm. The Indians finally galloped off to a safe distance, where our bullets could not reach them, and seemed to be holding a council. This was a lucky move for us, for it gave us an opportunity to reload our guns and pistols and prepare for the next charge of the enemy. During the brief cessation of hostilities Simpson extracted the arrow from Wood's shoulder, and put an immense quid of tobacco on the wound. Wood was then ready for business again.

The Indians did not give us a very long rest, for with another desperate charge, as if to ride over us, they came dashing toward the mule barricade. We gave them a hot reception from our yagers and revolvers. They could not stand or understand the rapidly repeating fire of the revolver, and we checked them again. They circled around us once more, and gave us a few parting shots as they rode off, leaving behind them another dead Indian and a horse.

For two hours afterward they did not seem to be doing anything but holding a council. We made good use of this time by digging up the ground inside the barricade with our knives, and throwing the loose earth around and over the mules, and we soon had a very respectable fortification. We were not troubled any more that day, but during the night the cunning rascals tried to burn us out by setting fire to the prairie. The buffalo grass was so short that the fire did not trouble us much, but the smoke concealed the Indians from our view, and they thought they could approach to us without being seen. We were aware of this, and kept a sharp lookout, being prepared all the time to receive them. They finally abandoned the idea of surprising us.

Next morning, bright and early, they gave us one more grand charge, and again we "stood them off." They then rode away half a mile or so, and formed a circle around us. Each man dismounted and sat down, as if to wait and starve us out. They had evidently seen the advance train pass on the morning of the previous day, and believed that we belonged to that outfit, and were trying to overtake it. They had no idea that another train was on its way after us.

Our hopes of escape from this unpleasant and perilous situation now depended upon the arrival of the rear train, and when we saw that the Indians were going to besiege us instead of renewing their attacks, we felt rather confident of receiving timely assistance. We had expected that the train would be along late in the afternoon of the previous day, and as the morning wore away we were somewhat anxious and uneasy at its nonarrival.

At last, about ten o'clock, we began to hear in the distance the loud and sharp reports of the big bull-whips, which were handled with great dexterity by the teamsters, and cracked like rifle shots. These were welcome sounds to us, as were the notes of the bagpipes to the besieged garrison at Lucknow when the re-enforcements were coming up, and the pipers were heard playing "The Campbells are Coming." In a few moments we saw the head wagon coming slowly over the ridge which had concealed the train from our view, and soon the whole outfit made its appearance. The Indians observed the approaching train, and assembling in a group, they held a short consultation. They then charged upon us once more, for the last time, and as they turned and dashed away over the prairie, we sent our farewell shots rattling after them. The teamsters, seeing the Indians and hearing the shots, came rushing forward to our assistance, but by that time the redskins had almost disappeared from view. The teamsters eagerly asked us a hundred questions concerning our fight, admired our fort, and praised our pluck. Simpson's remarkable presence of mind in planning the defense was the general topic of conversation among all the men.

When the teams came up we obtained some water and bandages with which to dress Wood's wound, which had become quite inflamed and painful, and we then put him into one of the wagons. Simpson and myself obtained a remount, bade good-by to our dead mules which had served us so well, and after collecting the ornaments and other plunder from the dead Indians, we left their bodies and bones to bleach on the prairie. The train moved on again, and we had no other adventures, except several exciting buffalo hunts on the South Platte near Plum Creek.

II

ROUNDING UP INDIANS

IN October, 1867, General Sheridan organized an expedition to operate against the Indians who infested the Republican River region. "Cody," said he, "I have decided to appoint you as guide and chief of scouts with the command. How does that suit you?"

"First rate, General, and thank you for the honor," I replied, as gracefully as I knew how.

The Dog Soldier Indians were a band of Cheyennes and unruly, turbulent members of other tribes, who would not enter into any treaty, or keep a treaty if they made one, and who had always refused to go upon a reservation. They were a warlike body of well-built, daring, and restless braves, and were determined to hold possession of the country in the vicinity of the Republican and Solomon rivers. They were called "Dog Soldiers" because they were principally Cheyennes—a name derived from the French *chien*, a dog.

On the 3d of October the Fifth Cavalry arrived at Fort Hays. General Sheridan, being anxious to punish the Indians who had lately fought General Forsyth, did not give the regiment much of a rest, and accordingly on the 5th of October it began its march for the Beaver Creek country. The first night we camped on the south fork of Big Creek, four miles west of Hays City. By this time I had become pretty well acquainted with Major Brown and Captain Sweetman, who invited me to mess with them on this expedition, and a jolly mess we had. There were other scouts in the command besides myself, and I particularly remember Tom Renahan, Hank Fields, and a character called "Nosey," on account of his long nose.

The next day we marched thirty miles, and late in the afternoon we came into camp on the south fork of the Solomon. At this encampment Colonel Royal asked me to go out and kill some buffaloes for the boys.

ROUNDING UP INDIANS

"All right, Colonel; send along a wagon or two to bring in the meat," I said.

"I am not in the habit of sending out my wagons until I know that there is something to be hauled in; kill your buffaloes first, and then I'll send out the wagons," was the Colonel's reply. I said no more, but went out on a hunt, and after a short absence returned and asked the Colonel to send out his wagons over the hill for the half-dozen buffaloes I had killed.

The following afternoon he again requested me to go out and get some fresh buffalo meat. I didn't ask him for any wagons this time, but rode out some distance, and coming up with a small herd I managed to get seven of them headed straight for the encampment, and instead of shooting them just then, I ran them at full speed right into the camp, and then killed them all, one after another, in rapid succession. Colonel Royal witnessed the whole proceeding, which puzzled him somewhat, as he could see no reason why I had not killed them on the prairie. He came up rather angrily, and demanded an explanation.

THE ADVENTURES OF BUFFALO BILL

"I can't allow any such business as this, Cody," said he. "What do you mean by it?"

"I didn't care about asking for any wagons this time, Colonel, so I thought I would make the buffaloes furnish their own transportation," was my reply. The Colonel saw the point in a moment, and had no more to say on the subject.

No Indians had been seen in the vicinity during the day, and Colonel Royal, having carefully posted his pickets, supposed everything was serene for the night. But before morning we were aroused from our slumbers by hearing shots fired, and immediately afterward one of the mounted pickets came galloping into camp, saying that there were Indians close at hand. The companies all fell into line, and were soon prepared and anxious to give the redskins battle; but as the men were yet new in the Indian country a great many of them were considerably excited. No Indians, however, made their appearance, and upon going to the picket-post where the picket said he had seen them none could be found, nor could any traces of them be discovered. The sentinel, who was an Irishman, insisted that there had certainly been redskins there.

"But you must be mistaken," said Colonel Royal.

"Upon me sowl, Colonel, I'm not. As shure ez me name's Pat Maloney, one of them redskins hit me on the head with a club, so he did," said Pat.

And so when morning came the mystery was further investigated, and was easily solved. Elk tracks were found in the vicinity, and it was undoubtedly a herd of elks that had frightened Pat. As he had turned to run he had gone under a limb of a tree against which he hit his head, and supposed he had been struck by a club in the hands of an Indian. It was hard to convince Pat, however, of the truth.

A three days' uninteresting march brought us to Beaver Creek, where we were camped, and from which point scouting parties were sent out in different directions. None of these, however, discovering Indians, they all returned to camp about the same time, finding it in a state of great excitement, it having been attacked a few hours previously by a party of Indians, who had succeeded in killing two men and in making off with sixty horses belonging to Company H.

That evening the command started on the trail of these Indian horse thieves, Major Brown with two companies and three days' rations pushing ahead in advance of the main command. Being unsuccessful, however, in overtaking the Indians, and getting nearly out of provisions—it being our eighteenth day out—the entire command marched toward the nearest railway point, and camped on the Saline River, distant three miles from Buffalo Tank. While waiting for supplies we received a new commanding officer, Brevet Major General E. A. Carr, who was the senior major of the regiment, and who ranked Colonel Royal. He brought with him the celebrated Forsyth scouts, who were commanded by Lieutenant Pepoon, a regular army officer.

The next morning, at an early hour, the command started out on a hunt for Indians. General Carr, having a pretty good idea where he would be most likely to find them, directed me to guide them by the nearest route to Elephant Rock on Beaver Creek. Upon arriving at the south fork of the Beaver on the second day's march, we discovered a large fresh Indian trail, which we hurriedly followed for a distance of eight miles, when suddenly we saw on the bluffs ahead of us quite a large number of Indians.

General Carr ordered Lieutenant Pepoon's scouts and Company M to the front. This company was commanded by Lieutenant Schinosky, a Frenchman by birth and reckless by nature. Having advanced his company nearly a mile ahead of the main command, about four hundred Indians suddenly charged down upon him and gave him a lively little fight, until he was supported by our full force. The Indians kept increasing in numbers all the while, until it was estimated that we were fighting from eight hundred to one thousand of them. The engagement became quite general, and several were killed and wounded on each side. The Indians were evidently fighting to give their families and village a chance to get away. We had undoubtedly surprised them with a larger force than they had expected to see in that part of the country. We fought them until dark, all the time driving them before us. At night they annoyed us considerably by firing down into our camp from the higher hills, and several times the command was ordered to dislodge them from their position and drive them back.

After having returned from one of these sallies, Major Brown, Captain Sweetman, Lieutenant Bache, and myself were taking supper together, when "whang!" came a bullet into Lieutenant Bache's plate, breaking a hole through it. The bullet came from the gun of one of the Indians, who had returned to the high bluff overlooking our camp. Major Brown declared it was a crack shot, because it broke the plate. We finished our supper without having any more such close calls.

At daylight next morning we struck out on the trail, and soon came to the spot where the Indians had camped the day before. We could see that their village was a very large one, consisting of about five hundred lodges; and we pushed forward rapidly from this point on the trail which ran back toward Prairie Dog Creek. About two o'clock we came in sight of the retreating village, and soon the warriors turned back to give us battle. They set fire to the prairie grass in front of us and on all sides in order to delay us as much as possible. We kept up a running fight for the remainder of the afternoon, and the Indians repeatedly attempted to lead us off the track of their flying village; but their trail was easily followed, as they were continually dropping tepee-poles, camp-kettles, robes, furs, and all heavy articles belonging to them. They were evidently scattering, and it finally became difficult for us to keep on the main trail. When darkness set in we went into camp, it being useless to try to follow the Indians after nightfall.

Next morning we were again on the trail. The Indians soon scattered in every direction, but we followed the main trail to the Republican River, where we made a cut-off, and then went north toward the Platte River. We found, however, that the Indians by traveling night and day had got a long start, and the General concluded that it was useless to follow them any farther.

The General told me that the next day's march would be toward the headwaters of the Beaver, and asked me the distance. I replied that it was about twenty-five miles, and he said he would make it the next day. Getting an early start in the morning, we struck out across the prairie, my position as guide being ahead of the advance guard. About two o'clock General Carr overtook me, and asked me how far I supposed it was to water. I thought it was about eight miles, although we could see no sign or indication of any stream in front.

"Pepoon's scouts say you are going in the wrong direction," said the General; "and in the way you are bearing it will be fifteen miles before you can strike any of the branches of the Beaver; and that when you do, you will find no water, for the Beavers are dry at this time of the year at that point."

"General, I think the scouts are mistaken," said I, "for the Beaver has more water near its head than it has below; and at the place where we will strike the stream we will find immense beaver dams, large enough and strong enough to cross the whole command, if you wish."

"Well, Cody, go ahead," said he; "I'll leave it to you; but remember that I don't want a dry camp."

"No danger of that," said I; and then I rode on, leaving him to return to the command. As I had predicted, we found water seven or eight miles farther on, where we came upon a beautiful little stream, a tributary of the Beaver, hidden in the hills. We had no difficulty in selecting a good halting-place, and obtaining fresh spring water and grass. The General, upon learning from me that the stream—which was only eight or nine miles long—had no name, took out his map and located it, and named it Cody's Creek, which name it still bears.

We pulled out early next morning for the Beaver, and when we were approaching the stream I rode on ahead of the advance guard in order to find the crossing. Just as I turned a bend of the creek, "bang!" went a shot, and down went my horse—myself with him. I disentangled myself, and jumped behind the dead body. Looking in the direction whence the shot had come I saw two Indians, and at once turned my gun loose on them, but in the excitement of the moment I missed my aim. They fired two or three more shots, and I returned the compliment, wounding one of their horses.

On the opposite side of the creek, going over the hill, I observed a few lodges moving rapidly away, and also some mounted warriors, who could see me, and who kept blazing away with their guns. The two Indians who had fired at me, and had killed my horse, were retreating across the creek on a beaver dam. I sent a few shots after them to accelerate their speed, and also fired at the ones on the other side of the stream. I was undecided as to whether it was best to run back to the command on foot or hold my position. I knew that within a few minutes the troops would come up, and I therefore decided to hold my position. The Indians, seeing that I was alone, turned, and charged down the hill, and were about to recross the creek to corral me, when the advance guard of the command put in an appearance on the ridge, and dashed forward to my rescue. The redskins whirled and made off.

When General Carr came up, he ordered Company I to go in pursuit of the band. I accompanied Lieutenant Brady, who commanded, and we had a running fight with the Indians, lasting several hours. We captured several head of their horses and most of their lodges. At night we returned to the command, which by this time had crossed the creek on the beaver dam.

We scouted for several days along the river, and had two or three lively skirmishes. Finally our supplies began to run low, and General Carr gave orders to return to Fort Wallace, which we reached three days afterward, and where we remained several days.

Very soon after, General Carr received orders from General Sheridan for a winter's campaign in the Canadian River country, instructing him to proceed at once to Fort Lyon, Colorado, and there to fit out for the expedition. Leaving Fort Wallace in November, 1868, we arrived at Fort Lyon in the latter part of the month without

special incident, and at once began our
preparations for invading the enemy's country. General Penrose had left his post three
weeks previously with a command of some
three hundred men. He had taken no
wagons with him, and his supply train was
composed only of pack mules. General
Carr was ordered to follow with supplies on
his trail and overtake him as soon as possible.
I was particularly anxious to catch up with
Penrose's command, as my old friend Wild
Bill was among his scouts. We followed the
trail very easily for the first three days, and
then we were caught in Freeze-Out Canyon
by a fearful snowstorm, which compelled
us to go into camp for a day. The ground
now being covered with snow, we found it
would be impossible to follow Penrose's
trail any farther, especially as he had left
no sign to indicate the direction he was going. General Carr sent for me, and said that
as it was very important that we should not
lose the trail, he wished that I would take
some scouts with me, and while the command remained in camp, push on as far as
possible, and see if I could not discover

some traces of Penrose or where he had camped at any time.

Accompanied by four men, I started out in the blinding snowstorm, taking a southerly direction. We rode twenty-four miles, and upon reaching a tributary of the Cimarron, we scouted up and down the stream for a few miles, and finally found one of Penrose's old camps. It was now late in the afternoon, and as the command would come up the next day, it was not necessary for all of us to return with the information to General Carr. So riding down into a sheltered place in the bend of the creek, we built a fire and broiled some venison from a deer which we had shot during the day, and after eating a substantial meal, I left the four men there while I returned to bring up the troops.

It was eleven o'clock at night when I got back to the camp. A light was still burning in the General's tent, he having remained awake, anxiously awaiting my return. He was glad to see me, and was overjoyed at the information I brought, for he had great fears concerning the safety of General Penrose.

43

The command took up its march next day for the Cimarron, and had a hard tramp of it on account of the snow having drifted to a great depth in many of the ravines, and in some places the teamsters had to shovel their way through. We arrived at the Cimarron at sundown, and went into camp. Upon looking around next morning, we found that Penrose, having been unencumbered by wagons, had kept on the west side of the Cimarron, and the country was so rough that it was impossible for us to stay on his trail with our wagons; but knowing that we would certainly follow down the river, General Carr concluded to take the best wagon route along the stream, which I discovered to be on the east side. Before we could make any headway with our wagon train we had to leave the river and get out on the divide. We were very fortunate that day in finding a splendid road for some distance, until we were all at once brought to a standstill on a high tableland, overlooking a beautiful winding creek that lay far below us in the valley. The question that troubled us was how we were to get the wagons down. We were now in the foothills of the Rattoon Mountains, and the bluff we were on was very steep.

"Cody, we're in a nice fix now," said General Carr.

"Oh, that's nothing," was my reply.

"But you can never take the train down," said he.

"Never you mind the train, General. You say you are looking for a good camp. How does that beautiful spot down in the valley suit you?" I asked him.

"That will do. I can easily descend with the cavalry, but how to get the wagons down there is a puzzler to me," said he.

"By the time you are located in your camp, your wagons shall be there," said I.

"All right, Cody, I'll leave it to you, as you seem to want to be boss," he replied, pleasantly. He at once ordered the command to dismount and lead the horses down the moutain side. The wagon train was a mile in the rear, and when it came up one of the drivers asked, "How are we going down there?"

45

"Run down, slide down, or fall down; any way to get down," said I.

"We can never do it; it's too steep; the wagons will run over the mules," said another wagon master.

"I guess not; the mules have got to keep out of the way," was my reply.

I told Wilson, the chief wagon master, to bring on his mess wagon, which was at the head of the train, and I would try the experiment at least. Wilson drove the team and wagon to the brink of the hill, and following my directions he brought out some extra chains with which we locked the wheels on each side, and then rough-locked them. We now started the wagon down the hill. The wheel horses—or rather the wheel mules—were good on the hold back, and we got along finely until we nearly reached the bottom, when the wagon crowded the mules so hard that they started on a run and galloped down into the valley and to the place where General Carr had located his camp. Three other wagons immediately followed in the same way, and in half an hour every wagon was in camp, with-

I DISENTANGLED MYSELF AND JUMPED BEHIND THE DEAD
BODY OF THE HORSE

out the least accident having occurred. It was indeed an exciting sight to see the six mule teams come straight down the mountain and finally break into a full run. At times it looked as if the wagons would turn a somersault and land on the mules.

This proved to be a lucky march for us, as far as gaining on Penrose was concerned; for the route he had taken on the west side of the stream turned out to be a bad one, and we went with our immense wagon train as far in one day as Penrose had in seven. His command had marched on to a plateau or high tableland so steep that not even a pack mule could descend it, and he was obliged to retrace his steps a long way, thus losing three days' time, as we afterward learned.

From this point on, for several days, we had no trouble in following Penrose's trail, which led us in a southeasterly direction toward the Canadian River. No Indians were seen, nor any signs of them found. One day, while riding in advance of the command down San Francisco Creek, I heard some one calling my name from a little bunch of willow brush on the opposite bank, and upon looking closely at the spot, I saw a negro.

"Sakes alive! Massa Bill, am dat you?" asked the man, whom I recognized as one of the colored soldiers of the Tenth Cavalry. I next heard him say to some one in the brush: "Come out o' heah. Dar's Massa Buffalo Bill." Then he sang out, "Massa Bill, is you got any hawdtack?"

"Nary a hardtack; but the wagons will be along presently, and then you can get all you want," said I.

"Dat's de best news I's heerd foah sixteen long days, Massa Bill," said he.

"Where's your command? Where's General Penrose?" I asked.

"I dun'no'," said the darky; "we got lost and we's been starvin' eber since."

By this time two other negroes had emerged from their place of concealment. They had deserted Penrose's command— which was out of rations and nearly in a starving condition—and were trying to make their way back to Fort Lyon. General Carr concluded, from what they could tell him, that General Penrose was somewhere on

Palladora Creek; but we could not learn anything definite, for they knew not where they were themselves.

Having learned that General Penrose's troops were in such bad shape, General Carr ordered Major Brown to start out the next morning with two companies of cavalry and fifty pack mules loaded with provisions, and to make all possible speed to reach and relieve the suffering soldiers. I accompanied this detachment, and on the third day out we found the half-famished soldiers camped on the Palladora. The camp presented a pitiful sight, indeed. For over two weeks the men had had only quarter rations, and were now nearly starved to death. Over two hundred horses and mules were lying dead, having died from fatigue and starvation. General Penrose, fearing that General Carr would not find him, had sent back a company of the Seventh Cavalry to Fort Lyon for supplies; but no word had as yet been heard from them. The rations which Major Brown brought to the command came none too soon, and were the means of saving many lives.

General Carr, upon arriving with his force, took command of all the troops, he being the senior officer and ranking General Penrose. After selecting a good camp, he unloaded the wagons and sent them back to Fort Lyon for fresh supplies. He then picked out five hundred of the best men and horses, and, taking his pack train with him, started south for the Canadian River, leaving the rest of the troops at the supply camp.

For several days we scouted along the Canadian River, but found no signs of Indians. General Carr then went back to his camp, and soon afterward our wagon train came in from Fort Lyon with a fresh load of provisions. At length, our horses and mules having become sufficiently recruited to return, we returned to Fort Lyon, arriving there in March, 1869, where the command was to rest and recruit for thirty days before proceeding to the Department of the Platte, whither it had been ordered.

III

Pursuing the Sioux

WHEN the Fifth Cavalry was ordered to the Department of the Platte, we moved from Fort Wallace down to Sheridan, and in a few days started on another expedition after the hostile Indians. The second day out, on reaching the North Fork of the Beaver and riding down the valley toward the stream, I suddenly discovered a large fresh Indian trail. On examination I found it to be scattered all over the valley on both sides of the creek, as if a very large village had recently passed that way. Judging from the size of the trail, I thought that there could not be less than four hundred lodges, or between twenty-five hundred and three thousand warriors, women, and children in the band. I galloped back to the command, distant about three miles, and reported the news to General Carr, who halted the regiment, and after consulting a few minutes, ordered me to select a ravine, or as low ground as possible, so that he could keep the troops out of sight until we could strike the creek.

We went into camp on the Beaver, and the General ordered Lieutenant Ward to take twelve men and myself and follow up the trail for several miles, and find out how fast the Indians were traveling. I was soon convinced, by the many camps they had made, that they were traveling slowly, and hunting as they journeyed. We went down the Beaver on this scout about twelve miles, keeping our horses well concealed under the banks of the creek, so as not to be discovered.

At this point, Lieutenant Ward and myself, leaving our horses behind us, crawled to the top of a high knoll, where we could have a good view for some miles distant down the stream. We peeped over the summit of the hill, and not over three miles away we could see a whole Indian village in plain sight, and thousands of ponies grazing around on the prairie. Looking over to our left, on the opposite side of the

creek we observed two or three parties of
Indians coming in, loaded down with buffalo meat.

"This is no place for us, Lieutenant," said
I; "I think we have important business at
the camp to attend to as soon as possible."

"I agree with you," said he, "and the
quicker we get there the better it will be
for us."

We quickly descended the hill and joined
the men below. Lieutenant Ward hurriedly
wrote a note to General Carr, and handing
it to a corporal, ordered him to make all
possible haste back to the command and de-
liver the message. The man started off on a
gallop, and Lieutenant Ward said, "We will
march slowly back until we meet the troops,
as I think the General will soon be here, for
he will start immediately upon receiving
my note."

In a few minutes we heard two or three
shots in the direction in which our dispatch
courier had gone, and soon after we saw him
come running around the bend of the creek,
pursued by four or five Indians. The Lieutenant, with his squad of soldiers and myself,

at once charged upon them, when they turned and ran across the stream.

"This will not do," said Lieutenant Ward; "the whole Indian village will now know that soldiers are near by."

"Lieutenant, give me that note, and I will take it to the General," said I.

He gladly handed me the dispatch, and spurring my horse I dashed up the creek. After having ridden a short distance, I observed another party of Indians, also going to the village with meat; but instead of waiting for them to fire upon me, I gave them a shot at long range. Seeing one man firing at them so boldly, it surprised them, and they did not know what to make of it. While they were thus considering, I got between them and our camp. By this time they had recovered from their surprise, and cutting their buffalo meat loose from their horses, they came after me at the top of their speed; but as their steeds were tired out, it did not take me long to leave them far in the rear.

I reached the command in less than an hour, delivered the dispatch to General Carr, and informed him of what I had seen.

PURSUING THE SIOUX

He instantly had the bugler sound "boots and saddles," and all the troops, with the exception of two companies which we left to guard the train, were soon galloping in the direction of the Indian camp.

We had ridden about three miles, when we met Lieutenant Ward, who was coming slowly toward us. He reported that he had run into a party of Indian buffalo hunters, and had killed one of the number, and had had one of his horses wounded. We immediately pushed forward, and after marching about five miles came within sight of hundreds of mounted Indians advancing up the creek to meet us. They formed a complete line in front of us. General Carr, being desirous of striking their village, ordered the troops to charge, break through their line, and keep straight on. This movement would no doubt have been successfully accomplished had it not been for the rattle-brained and dare-devil French Lieutenant Schinosky, commanding Company B, who, misunderstanding General Carr's orders, charged upon some Indians at the left, while the rest of the command dashed through the

THE ADVENTURES OF BUFFALO BILL

enemy's line, and was keeping straight on, when it was observed that Schinosky and his company were surrounded by four or five hundred Indians. The General, to save the company, was obliged to sound a halt and charge back to the rescue. The company during this short fight had several men and quite a number of horses killed.

All this took up valuable time, and night was coming on. The Indians were fighting desperately to keep us from reaching their village, which, being informed by couriers of what was taking place, was packing up and getting away. During that afternoon it was all that we could do to hold our own in fighting the mounted warriors, who were in our front and contesting every inch of the ground. The General had left word for our wagon train to follow up with its escort of two companies, but as it had not made its appearance, he entertained some fears that it had been surrounded, and to prevent the possible loss of the supply train we had to go back and look for it. About nine o'clock that evening we found it and went into camp for the night.

PURSUING THE SIOUX

Early the next day we broke camp and passed down the creek, but there was not an Indian to be seen. They had all disappeared and gone on with their village. Two miles farther we came to where a village had been located, and here we found nearly everything belonging to or pertaining to an Indian camp, which had been left in the great hurry to get away. These articles were all gathered up and burned. We then pushed out on the trail as fast as possible. It led us to the northeast toward the Republican; but as the Indians had a night the start of us, we entertained but little hope of overtaking them that day. Upon reaching the Republican in the afternoon the General called a halt, and as the trail was running more to the east, he concluded to send his wagon train on to Fort McPherson by the most direct route, while he would follow on the trail of the redskins.

Next morning at daylight we again pulled out, and were evidently gaining rapidly on the Indians, for we could occasionally see them in the distance. About eleven o'clock that day, while Major Babcock was ahead of the main command with his company, and while we were crossing a deep ravine, we were surprised by about three hundred warriors, who commenced a lively fire upon us. Galloping out of the ravine on to the rough prairie, the men dismounted and returned the fire. We soon succeeded in driving the Indians before us and were so close to them at one time that they abandoned and threw away nearly all their lodges and camp equipage, and everything that had any considerable weight. They left behind them their played-out horses, and for miles we could see Indian furniture strewn along in every direction. The trail became divided, and the Indians scattered in small bodies all over the prairie. As night was approaching and our horses were about giving out, a halt was called. A company was detailed to collect all the Indian horses running loose over the country, and to burn the other Indian property.

The command being nearly out of rations, I was sent to the nearest point, old Fort Kearny, about sixty miles distant, for supplies.

PURSUING THE SIOUX

Shortly after we reached Fort McPherson, which continued to be the headquarters of the Fifth Cavalry for some time, we fitted out for a new expedition to the Republican River country, and were re-enforced by three companies of the celebrated Pawnee Indian scouts, commanded by Major Frank North. General Carr recommended at this time to General Augur, who was in command of the department, that I be made chief of scouts in the Department of the Platte, and informed me that in this position I would receive higher wages than I had been getting in the Department of the Missouri. This appointment I had not asked for.

I made the acquaintance of Major Frank North, and I found him and his officers perfect gentlemen, and we were all good friends from the very start. The Pawnee scouts had made quite a reputation for themselves, as they had performed brave and valuable services in fighting against the Sioux, whose bitter enemies they were; being thoroughly acquainted with the Republican and Beaver country, I was glad that they were to be with the expedition, and my expectation of the aid they would render was not disappointed.

During our stay at Fort McPherson I made the acquaintance of Lieutenant George P. Belden, known as the "White Chief." I found him to be an intelligent, dashing fellow, a splendid rider, and an excellent shot. An hour after our introduction he challenged me for a rifle match, the preliminaries of which were soon arranged. We were to shoot ten shots each for fifty dollars, at two hundred yards, off-hand. Belden was to use a Henry rifle, while I was to shoot my old "Lucretia." This match I won, and then Belden proposed to shoot a one-hundred-yard match, as I was shooting over his distance. In this match Belden was victorious. We were now even, and we stopped right there.

While we were at this post General Augur and several of his officers paid us a visit for the purpose of reviewing the command. The regiment turned out in fine style and showed themselves to be well-drilled soldiers, thoroughly understanding military tactics. The

Pawnee scouts were also reviewed, and it was very amusing to see them in their full regular uniform. They had been furnished a regulation cavalry uniform, and on this parade some of them had their heavy overcoats on, others their large black hats, with all the brass accouterments attached; some of them were minus pantaloons, and only wore a breech-clout. Others wore regulation pantaloons, but no shirts, and were bareheaded; others again had the seat of the pantaloons cut out, leaving only leggings; but for all this they seemed to understand the drill remarkably well for Indians. The commands, of course, were given to them in their own language by Major North, who could talk it as well as any full-blooded Pawnee. The Indians were well mounted, and felt proud and elated because they had been made United States soldiers. Major North had for years complete control over these Indians, and could do more with them than any man living. That evening, after the parade was over, the officers and quite a number of ladies visited a grand Indian dance given by the Pawnees, and of all the

Indians I have seen, their dances excel those of any other tribe.

Next day the command started. When encamped, several days after, on the Republican River, near the mouth of the Beaver, we heard the whoops of Indians, followed by shots in the vicinity of the mule herd, which had been taken down to water. One of the herders came dashing into camp with an arrow sticking in him. My horse was close at hand, and mounting him bareback, I at once dashed off after the mule herd, which had been stampeded. I supposed certainly that I would be the first man on the ground, but I was mistaken, however, for the Pawnee Indians, unlike regular soldiers, had not waited to receive orders from their officers, but had jumped on their ponies without bridles or saddles, and placing ropes in their mouths, had dashed off in the direction whence the shots came, and had got there ahead of me. It proved to be a party of about fifty Sioux who had endeavored to stampede our mules, and it took them by surprise to see their inveterate enemies, the Pawnees, coming at full gallop at them.

PURSUING THE SIOUX

They were not aware that the Pawnees were with the command, and as they knew it would take regular soldiers some time to turn out, they thought they would have ample opportunity to secure the herd before the troops could give chase.

We had a running fight of fifteen miles, and several of the enemy were killed. During this chase I was mounted on an excellent horse, which Colonel Royal had picked out for me, and for the first mile or two I was in advance of the Pawnees. Presently a Pawnee shot by me like an arrow, and I could not help admiring the horse he was riding. Seeing that he possessed rare running qualities, I determined to get possession of the animal in some way. It was a large buckskin or yellow horse, and I took a careful view of him, so that I would know him when I returned to camp.

After the chase was over I rode up to Major North and inquired about the buckskin horse.

"Oh yes," said the Major; "that is one of our favorite steeds."

"What chance is there to trade for him?" I asked.

"It is a government horse," said he, "and the Indian who is riding him is very much attached to the animal."

"I have fallen in love with the horse myself," said I, "and I would like to know if you have any objections to my trading for him if I can arrange it satisfactorily with the Indians?"

He replied, "None whatever, and I will help you to do it; you can give the Indian another horse in his place."

A few days after this I persuaded the Indian, by making him several presents, to trade horses with me, and in this way I became the owner of the buckskin steed; not as my own property, however, but as a government horse that I could ride. I gave him the name of "Buckskin Joe," and he proved to be a fine buffalo hunter. In the winter of 1872, after I had left Fort McPherson, Buckskin Joe was condemned and sold at public sale, and was bought by Dave Perry, at North Platte, who in 1877 presented him to me, and I owned him until his death in 1879.

PURSUING THE SIOUX

The command scouted several days up the Beaver and Prairie Dog rivers, occasionally having running fights with way parties of Indians, but did not succeed in getting them into a general battle. At the end of twenty days we found ourselves back on the Republican.

Hitherto the Pawnees had not taken much interest in me, but while at this camp I gained their respect and admiration by showing them how I killed buffaloes. Although the Pawnees were excellent buffalo hunters, for Indians, I have never seen one of them kill more than four or five in a single run. A number of them generally surround the herd and then dash in upon them, and in this way each one kills from one to four buffaloes. I had gone out in company with Major North and some of the officers, and saw them make a "surround." Twenty of the Pawness circled a herd and succeeded in killing only thirty-two.

While they were cutting up the animals another herd appeared in sight. The Indians were preparing to surround it, when I asked Major North to keep them back and let me show them what I could do. He accordingly informed the Indians of my wish, and they readily consented to let me have the opportunity. I had learned that Buckskin Joe was an excellent buffalo horse, and felt confident that I would astonish the natives. Galloping in among the buffaloes, I certainly did so by killing thirty-six in less than a half-mile run. At nearly every shot I killed a buffalo, stringing the dead animals out on the prairie, not over fifty feet apart. This manner of killing was greatly admired by the Indians, who called me a big chief, and from that time on I stood high in their estimation.

On leaving camp the command took a westward course up the Republican, and Major North, with two companies of cavalry, under the command of Colonel Royal, made a scout to the north of the river. Shortly after we had gone into camp, on the Black Tail Deer Fork, we observed a band of Indians coming over the prairie at full gallop, singing and yelling and waving their lances and long poles. At first we supposed them to be Sioux, and all was excitement for a few moments. We noticed, however, that our Pawnee Indians made no hostile demonstrations or preparations toward going out to fight them, but began singing and yelling themselves. Captain Lute North stepped up to General Carr and said: "General, those are our men who are coming, and they have had a fight. That is the way they act when they come back from a battle and have taken any scalps."

The Pawnees came into camp on the run. Captain North, calling to one of them, a sergeant, soon found out that they had run across a party of Sioux who were following a large Indian trail. These Indians had evidently been in a fight, for two or three of them had been wounded, and they were conveying the injured persons on *travoix*. The Pawnees had "jumped" them, and had killed three or four after a sharp fight, in which much ammunition was expended.

Next morning the command, at an early hour, started out to take up this Indian trail, which they followed for two days as rapidly as possible, it becoming evident from the many camp fires which we passed that we were gaining on the Indians. Wherever they had encamped we found the print of a woman's shoe, and we concluded that they had with them some white captive. This made us all the more anxious to overtake them, and General Carr selected all his best horses which could stand a long run, and gave orders for the wagon train to follow as fast as possible, while he pushed ahead on a forced march. At the same time I was ordered to pick out five or six of the best Pawnees and go in advance of the command, keeping ten or twelve miles ahead on the trail, so that when we overtook the Indians we could find out the location of their camp, and send word to the troops before they came in sight, thus affording ample time to arrange a plan for the capture of the village.

After having gone about ten miles in advance of the regiment, we began to move very cautiously, as we were now evidently nearing the Indians. We looked carefully over the summits of the hills before exposing ourselves to plain view, and at last we discovered the village, encamped in the sand hills south of the South Platte River at Summit Springs. Here I left the Pawnee scouts to keep watch, while I went back and informed General Carr that the Indians were in sight.

The General at once ordered his men to tighten their saddles and otherwise prepare for action. Soon all was excitement among the officers and soldiers, every one being anxious to charge the village. I now changed my horse for old Buckskin Joe, who had been led for me thus far, and was comparatively fresh. Acting on my suggestion, the General made a circuit to the north, believing that if the Indians had their scouts out they would naturally be watching in the direction whence they had come. When we had passed the Indians, and were between them and the Platte River, we turned toward the left and started toward the village.

By this manœuver we had avoided discovery by the Sioux scouts, and we were confident of giving them a complete surprise. Keeping the command wholly out of sight until we were within a mile of the Indians, the General halted the advance guard until all closed up, and then issued an order that when he sounded the charge the whole command was to rush into the village.

As we halted on the top of the hill overlooking the camp of unsuspecting Indians, General Carr called out to his bugler, "Sound the charge!"

The bugler for a moment became intensely excited, and actually forgot the notes. The General again sang out, "Sound the charge!" and yet the bugler was unable to obey the command. Quartermaster Hays—who had obtained permission to accompany the expedition—was riding near the General, and comprehending the dilemma of the man, rushed up to him, jerked the bugle from his hands, and sounded the charge himself in clear, distinct notes. As the troops rushed forward, he threw the bugle away, then drawing his pistols, was among the first men that entered the village.

The Indians had just driven up their horses, and were preparing to make a move of the camp, when they saw the soldiers coming down upon them. A great many of them succeeded in jumping upon their ponies and, leaving everything behind them, advanced out of the village and prepared to meet the charge; but, upon second thought, they quickly concluded that it was useless to try to check us, and those who were mounted rapidly rode away, while the others on foot fled for safety to the neighboring hills. We went through their village, shooting right and left at everything we saw. The Pawnees, the regular soldiers, and officers were all mixed up together, and the Sioux were flying in every direction.

The pursuit continued until darkness made it impossible to longer follow the Indians, who had scattered and were leading off in every direction like a brood of young quails. The expedition went into camp along the South Platte, much exhausted by so long a chase, and though very tired, every trooper seemed anxious for the morrow.

It was nearly sunrise when "boots and saddles" was sounded, breakfast having been disposed of at break of day. The command started in a most seasonable time, but finding that the trail was all broken up, it was deemed advisable to separate into companies, each to follow a different trail.

The company which I headed struck out toward the northwest, over a route indicating the march of about one hundred Indians, and followed this for nearly two days. At a short bend of the Platte a new trail was discovered leading into the one the company was following, and at this point it was evident that a junction had been made. Farther along evidences of a reunion of the entire village increased, and now it began to appear that further pursuit would be somewhat hazardous, owing to the largely increased force of Indians. But there were plenty of brave men in the company, and nearly all were anxious to meet the Indians, however great their numbers might be. This anxiety was appeased on the third day, when a party of about six hundred Sioux was discovered riding in close ranks near the Platte. The discovery was mutual, and there was immediate preparation for battle on both sides. Owing to the overwhelming force of Indians, extreme caution became necessary, and instead of advancing boldly, the soldiers sought advantageous ground. Seeing this, the Indians became convinced that there had been a division in General Carr's command, and that the company before them was a fragmentary part of the expedition. They therefore assumed the aggressive, charging us until we were compelled to retire to a ravine and act on the defensive. The attack was made with such caution that the soldiers fell back without undue haste, and had ample opportunity to secure their horses in the natural pit, which was a ravine that during wet seasons formed a branch of the Platte.

After circling about the soldiers with a view of measuring their full strength, the Indians, comprehending how small was the number, made a desperate charge from two sides, getting so near us that several of the soldiers were badly wounded by arrows. But the Indians were received with such withering fire that they fell back in confusion, leaving twenty of their warriors on the ground. Another charge resulted like the first, with heavy loss to the redskins, which so discouraged them that they drew off and held a long council. After discussing the situation among themselves, they separated, one body making off as though they intended to leave; but I understood their motions too well to allow the soldiers to be deceived.

The Indians that remained again began to ride in a circle around us, but maintained a safe distance out of rifle range. Seeing an especially well-mounted Indian riding at the head of a squad, passing around in the same circle more than a dozen times, I decided to take my chances for dismounting the chief (as he proved to be), and to accomplish this purpose I crawled on my hands and knees three hundred yards up the ravine, stopping at a point which I considered would be in range of the Indian when he should again make the circuit. My judgment proved correct, for soon the Indian was seen loping his pony through the grass, and as he slackened speed to cross the ravine I rose up and fired, the aim being so well taken that the chief tumbled to the ground, while his horse, after running a few hundred yards, approached the soldiers, one of whom ran out and caught hold of the long lariat attached to the bridle, and thus secured the animal. When I returned to the company, all of whom had witnessed my feat of killing an Indian at a range of fully four hundred yards, by general consent the horse of my victim was given to me.

This Indian whom I killed proved to be Tall Bull, one of the most cunning and able chiefs the Sioux ever had, and his death so affected the Indians that they at once retreated without further attempt to dislodge us.

Some days after this occurrence General Carr's command was brought together again and had an engagement with the Sioux, in which more than three hundred warriors and a large number of ponies were captured, together with several hundred squaws, among the latter being Tall Bull's widow, who told with pathetic interest how the Prairie Chief had killed her husband. But instead of being moved with hatred against me, as most civilized women would have been under like circumstances, she regarded me with special favor, and esteemed it quite an honor that her husband, a great warrior himself, should have met his death at my hands.

IV

My Duel with Yellow Hand

WHEN the news of the terrible massacre of Custer was learned, preparations were immediately made to avenge his death. The whole Cheyenne and Sioux tribes were in revolt, and a lively, if not very dangerous, campaign was in prospective. Two days before receipt of the news of the massacre, Colonel Stanton, who was with the Fifth Cavalry, had been sent to Red Cloud agency, and on the evening of the receipt of news of the Custer fight a scout arrived in our camp with a message from the Colonel, informing General Merritt that eight hundred Cheyenne warriors had that day left Red Cloud agency to join Sitting Bull's hostile forces in the Big Horn country.

Notwithstanding the instructions to proceed immediately to join General Crook by the way of Fort Fetterman, General Merritt took the responsibility of endeavoring to intercept the Cheyennes, and, as the sequel shows, he performed a very important service.

He selected five hundred men and horses, and in two hours we were making a forced march back to Hat, or War-Bonnet Creek, the intention being to reach the main Indian trail running to the north across that creek before the Cheyennes could get there. We arrived there the next night, and at daylight the following morning, July 17, 1876, I went out on a scout, and found that the Indians had not yet crossed the creek. On my way back to the command I discovered a large party of Indians, which proved to be the Cheyennes, coming up from the south, and I hurried to the camp with this important information.

The cavalrymen quietly mounted their horses and were ordered to remain out of sight, while General Merritt, accompanied by two or three aids and myself, went out on a little tour of observation to a neighboring hill, from the summit of which we saw that the Indians were approaching almost directly toward us. Presently fifteen or twenty of them dashed off to the west, in the direction from which we had come the night before; and upon closer observation with our field glasses we discovered two mounted soldiers, evidently carrying dispatches for us, pushing forward on our trail.

The Indians were evidently trying to intercept these two men, and General Merritt feared that they would accomplish their object. He did not think it advisable to send out any soldiers to the assistance of the couriers, for fear that they would show to the Indians that there were troops in the vicinity who were waiting for them. I finally suggested that the best plan was to wait until the couriers came closer to the command, and then, just as the Indians were about to charge, to let me take the scouts and cut them off from the main body of the Cheyennes who were coming over the divide.

"All right, Cody," said the General. "If you can do that, go ahead."

I rushed back to the command, jumped

on my horse, picked out fifteen men, and returned with them to the point of observation. I told General Merritt to give us the word to start out at the proper time, and presently he sang out:

"Go in now, Cody, and be quick about it. They are going to charge on the couriers."

The two messengers were not over four hundred yards from us, and the Indians were only about two hundred yards behind them. We instantly dashed over the bluffs, and advanced on a gallop toward the Indians. A running fight lasted several minutes, during which we drove the enemy some little distance and killed three of their number. The rest of them rode off toward the main body, which had come into plain sight and halted, upon seeing the skirmish that was going on. We were about half a mile from General Merritt, and the Indians whom we were chasing suddenly turned upon us, and another lively skirmish took place. One of the Indians, who was handsomely decorated with all the ornaments usually worn by a war chief when engaged in a fight, sang out to me, in his own tongue, "I know you, Pa-he-haska; if you want to fight, come ahead and fight me."

The chief was riding his horse back and forth in front of his men as if to banter me, and I concluded to accept the challenge. I galloped toward him for fifty yards, and he advanced toward me about the same distance, both of us riding at full speed, and then, when we were only about thirty yards apart, I raised my rifle and fired; his horse fell to the ground, having been killed by a bullet. Almost at the same moment my own horse went down, he having stepped into a gopher hole. The fall did not hurt me much, and I instantly sprang to my feet. The Indian had also recovered himself, and we were now both on foot, and not more than twenty paces apart. We fired at each other simultaneously. My usual luck did not desert me on this occasion, for his bullet missed me, while mine struck him in the breast. He reeled and fell, but before he had fairly touched the ground I was upon him, knife in hand, and had driven the keen-edged weapon to its hilt in his heart. Jerking his war bonnet off, I scientifically scalped him in about five seconds.

The whole affair from beginning to end occupied but little time, and the Indians, seeing that I was some little distance from my company, now came charging down upon me from a hill, in hopes of cutting me off. General Merritt had witnessed the duel, and realizing the danger I was in, ordered Colonel Mason with Company K to hurry to my rescue. The order came none too soon, for had it been one minute later I would have had not less than two hundred Indians upon me. As the soldiers came up I swung the Indian chieftain's topknot and bonnet in the air and shouted, "the first scalp for Custer."

General Merritt, seeing that he could not now ambush the Indians, ordered the whole regiment to charge upon them. They made a stubborn resistance for a little while, but it was no use for any eight hundred, or even sixteen hundred, Indians to try to check a charge of the gallant old Fifth Cavalry, and they soon came to that conclusion, and began a running retreat toward Red Cloud agency.

For thirty-five miles we drove them, pushing them so hard that they were obliged to abandon their loose horses, their camp equipage, and everything else. We drove them into the agency, and followed in ourselves, notwithstanding the possibility of our having to encounter the thousands of Indians at that point. We were uncertain whether or not the agency Indians had determined to follow the example of the Cheyennes and strike out upon the warpath; but that made no difference with the Fifth Cavalry, for they would have fought them all if necessary. It was dark when we rode into the agency, where we found thousands of Indians collected together; but they manifested no disposition to fight.

While at the agency I learned the name of the Indian chief whom I had killed that morning; it was Yellow Hand, a son of old Cut Nose, a leading chief of the Cheyennes. Cut Nose having learned that I had killed his son, sent a white interpreter to me with a message to the effect that he would give me four mules if I would turn over to him Yellow Hand's war-bonnet, guns, pistols, ornaments, and other paraphernalia which I had captured. I sent back word to the old gentleman that it would give me pleasure to accommodate him, but I could not do it this time.

The next morning we started to join General Crook, who was camped near the foot of Cloud Peak in the Big Horn Mountains, awaiting the arrival of the Fifth Cavalry before proceeding against the Sioux, who were somewhere near the head of the Little Big Horn—as his scouts informed him. We made rapid marches, and reached General Crook's camp on Goose Creek about the 3d of August.

At this camp I met many old friends, among whom was Colonel Royal, who had received his promotion to the lieutenant colonelcy of the Third Cavalry. He introduced me to General Crook, whom I had never met before, but of whom I had often heard. He also introduced me to the General's chief guide, Frank Grouard, a halfbreed, who had lived six years with Sitting Bull, and knew the country thoroughly.

We remained in this camp only one day,

and the whole troop pulled out for the
Tongue River, leaving our wagons behind,
but taking with us a large pack train. We
marched down the Tongue River for two
days, thence in a westerly direction over to
the Rosebud, where we struck the main Indian trail leading down this stream. From
the size of the trail, which appeared to be
about four days old, we estimated that there
must have been in the neighborhood of seven
thousand Indians in the war party.

For two or three days we pushed on, but
we did not seem to gain much on the Indians, as they were evidently making about
the same marches that we were. On the
fourth or fifth morning of our pursuit, I rode
ahead of the command about ten miles, and
mounting a hill, I scanned the country far
and wide with my field glass, and discovered
a column of dust rising about ten miles
farther down the creek, and soon I noticed a
body of men marching toward me that at
first I believed to be the Indians of whom
we were in pursuit; but subsequently they
proved to be General Terry's command. I
sent back word to that effect to General

Crook by a scout who had accompanied me, but after he had departed I observed a band of Indians on the opposite side of the creek, and also another party directly in front of me. This led me to believe that I had made a mistake. But shortly afterward my attention was attracted by the appearance of a body of soldiers who were forming into a skirmish line and then I became convinced that it was General Terry's command, after all, and that the redskins whom I had seen were some of his friendly Indian scouts, who had mistaken me for a Sioux, and fled back to their command terribly excited, shouting, "The Sioux are coming!"

General Terry at once came to the post, and ordered the Seventh Cavalry to form line of battle across the Rosebud; he also ordered up his artillery and had them prepare for action, doubtless dreading another "Custer massacre." I afterward learned that the Indian had seen the dust raised by General Crook's forces, and had reported that the Sioux were coming.

These manœuvers I witnessed from my position with considerable amusement, thinking the command must be badly demoralized when one man could cause a whole army to form line of battle and prepare for action. Having enjoyed the situation to my heart's content, I galloped down toward the skirmish line, waving my hat, and when within about one hundred yards of the troops, Colonel Weir, of the Seventh Cavalry, galloped out and met me. He recognized me at once, and accompanied me inside the line; then he sang out: "Boys, here's Buffalo Bill. Some of you old soldiers know him; give him a cheer!" Thereupon the regiment gave three rousing cheers, and it was followed up all along the line.

Colonel Weir presented me to General Terry, and in answer to his question I informed him that the alarm of Indians had been a false one, as the dust seen by his scouts was caused by General Crook's troops. General Terry thereupon rode forward to meet General Crook, and I accompanied him at his request. That night both commands went into camp on the Rosebud. General Terry had his wagon train with him, and everything to make life comfort-

able on an Indian campaign. He had large
wall tents and portable beds to sleep in, and
commodious hospital tents for dining rooms.
His camp looked very comfortable and at-
tractive, and presented a great contrast to
that of General Crook, who had for his headquarters only one small fly tent, and whose
cooking utensils consisted of a quart cup—
in which he made his coffee himself—and a
stick upon which he broiled his bacon.
When I compared the two camps, I came
to the conclusion that General Crook was
an Indian-fighter; for it was evident that
he had learned that to follow and fight Indians a body of men must travel lightly, and
not be detained by a wagon train or heavy
luggage of any kind.

That evening General Terry ordered
General Miles to take his regiment, the
Fifth Infantry, and return by a forced
march to Yellowstone, and proceed down
the river by steamboat to the mouth of the
Powder River, to intercept the Indians, in
case they attempted to cross the Yellowstone. General Miles made a forced march
that night of thirty-five miles, which was

splendid traveling for an infantry regiment through a mountainous country.

Generals Crook and Terry spent that evening and the next day in council, and on the following morning both commands moved out on the Indian trail. Although General Terry was the senior officer, he did not assume command of both expeditions, but left General Crook in command of his own troops, although they operated together. We crossed the Tongue River to Powder River, and proceeded down the latter stream to a point twenty miles from its junction with the Yellowstone, where the Indian trail turned to the southeast in the direction of the Black Hills. The two commands now being nearly out of supplies, the trail was abandoned, and the troops kept on down Powder River to its confluence with the Yellowstone, and remained there several days. Here we met General Miles, who reported that no Indians had as yet crossed the Yellowstone. Several steamboats soon arrived with a large quantity of supplies, and once more the "Boys in Blue" were made happy.

One evening, while we were in camp on

the Yellowstone at the mouth of Powder River, I was informed that the commanding officer had selected Louis Richard, a half-breed, and myself to accompany General Miles on a scouting expedition on the steamer *Far West,* down the Yellowstone as far as Glendive Creek. We were to ride on the pilot house and keep a sharp lookout on both sides of the river for Indian trails that might have crossed the stream. The idea of scouting on a steamboat was indeed a novel one to me, and I anticipated a pleasant trip.

At daylight next morning we reported on board the steamer to General Miles, who had with him four or five companies of his regiment. We were somewhat surprised when he asked us where our horses were, as we had not supposed that horses would be needed if the scouting was to be done on the steamer. He said we might need them before we got back, and thereupon we had the animals brought on board. In a few minutes we were booming down the river at the rate of about twenty miles an hour.

The steamer *Far West* was commanded by Captain Grant Marsh, whom I found to be an interesting character. I had often heard of him, for he was, and is yet, one of the best-known river captains in the country. He it was who, with his steamer *Far West,* transported the wounded men from the battle of the Little Big Horn to Fort Abraham Lincoln on the Missouri River, and on that trip he made the fastest steamboat time on record. He was a skillful and experienced pilot, handling his boat with remarkable dexterity.

While Richard and myself were at our stations on the pilot house, the steamer, with a full head of steam, went flying past islands, around bends, over sand bars, at a rate that was exhilarating. Presently I thought I could see horses grazing in a distant bend of the river, and I reported the fact to General Miles, who asked Captain Marsh if he could land the boat near a large tree which he pointed out to him. "Yes, sir; I can land her there, and make her climb the tree if necessary," said he.

On reaching the spot designated, General Miles ordered two companies ashore, while Richard and myself were instructed to take our horses off the boat and push out as rapidly as possible to see if there were Indians in the vicinity. While we were getting ashore, Captain Marsh remarked that if there were only a good heavy dew on the grass he would shoot the steamer ashore, and take us on the scout without the trouble of leaving the boat.

It was a false alarm, however, as the objects we had seen proved to be Indian graves. Quite a large number of braves, who had probably been killed in some battle, were laid on scaffolds, according to the Indian custom, and some of their clothing had been torn from the bodies by the wolves and was waving in the air.

On arriving at Glendive Creek we found that Colonel Rice and his company of the Fifth Infantry, who had been sent there by General Miles, had built quite a good little fort with their trowel-bayonets, a weapon which Colonel Rice was the inventor of, and which is, by the way, a very useful implement of war, as it can be used for a shovel in throwing up intrenchments, and can be profitably utilized in several other ways.

On the day previous to our arrival Colonel Rice had a fight with a party of Indians, and had killed two or three of them at long range with his Rodman cannon.

The *Far West* was to remain at Glendive overnight, and General Miles wished to send dispatches back to General Terry at once. At his request I took the dispatches, and rode seventy-five miles that night through the bad lands of the Yellowstone, and reached General Terry's camp next morning, after having nearly broken my neck a dozen times or more.

There being but little prospect of any more fighting, I determined to go East as soon as possible to engage in other pursuits. So I started down the river on the steamer *Yellowstone, en route* to Fort Beaufort. On the same morning Generals Terry and Crook pulled out for Powder River, to take up the old Indian trail which we had left.

The steamer had proceeded down the stream about twenty miles when it was met by another boat on its way up the river, having on board General Whistler and some fresh troops for General Terry's command.

Both boats landed, and I met several old friends among the soldiers.

General Whistler, upon learning that General Terry had left the Yellowstone, asked me to carry to him some important dispatches from General Sheridan, and although I objected, he insisted upon my performing this duty, saying that it would only detain me a few hours longer; as an extra inducement he offered me the use of his own thoroughbred horse, which was on the boat. I finally consented to go, and was soon speeding over the rough and hilly country toward Powder River, and delivered the dispatches to General Terry the same evening. General Whistler's horse, although a good animal, was not used to such hard riding, and was far more exhausted by the journey than I was.

After I had taken a lunch, General Terry asked me if I would carry some dispatches back to General Whistler, and I replied that I would. Captain Smith, General Terry's aid-de-camp, offered me his horse for the trip, and it proved to be an excellent animal; for I rode him that same night forty miles over the bad lands in four hours, and reached General Whistler's steamboat at one o'clock. During my absence the Indians had made their appearance on the different hills of the vicinity, and the troops from the boat had had several skirmishes with them. When General Whistler had finished reading the dispatches, he said: "Cody, I want to send some information to General Terry concerning the Indians who have been skirmishing around here all day. I have been trying all the evening long to induce some one to carry my dispatches to him, but no one seems willing to undertake the trip, and I have got to fall back on you. It is asking a great deal, I know, as you have just ridden eighty miles; but it is a case of necessity, and if you'll go, Cody, I'll see that you are well paid for it."

"Never mind about the pay," said I, "but get your dispatches ready and I'll start at once."

In a few minutes he handed me the package, and, mounting the same horse which I had ridden from General Terry's camp, I struck out for my destination. It was two o'clock in the morning when I left the boat, and at eight o'clock I rode into General Terry's camp, just as he was about to march, having made one hundred and twenty miles in twenty-two hours.

General Terry, after reading the dispatches, halted his command, and then rode on and overtook General Crook, with whom he held a council; the result was that Crook's command moved on in the direction which they had been pursuing, while Terry's forces marched back to the Yellowstone and crossed the river on steamboats. At the urgent request of General Terry I accompanied the command on a scout in the direction of the Dry Fork of the Missouri, where it was expected we would strike some Indians.

The first march out from the Yellowstone was made in the night, as we wished to get into the hills without being discovered by the Sioux scouts. After marching three days a little to the east of north, we reached the buffalo range and discovered fresh signs of Indians, who had evidently been killing buffaloes. General Terry now called on me to carry dispatches to Colonel Rice, who was still encamped at the mouth of Glendive Creek, on the Yellowstone—distant about eighty miles from us.

Night had set in with a storm, and a drizzling rain was falling when, at ten o'clock, I started on this ride through a section of country with which I was entirely unacquainted. I traveled through the darkness a distance of about thirty-five miles, and at daylight I rode into a secluded spot at the head of a ravine where stood a bunch of ash trees, and there I concluded to remain till night, for I considered it a dangerous undertaking to cross the wide prairies in broad daylight —especially as my horse was a poor one. I accordingly unsaddled my animal and ate a hearty breakfast of bacon and hardtack which I had stored in the saddle pockets; then, after taking a smoke, I lay down to sleep, with my saddle for a pillow. In a few minutes I was in the land of dreams.

After sleeping some time—I cannot tell how long—I was suddenly awakened by a roaring, rumbling sound. I instantly seized my gun, sprang to my horse, and hurriedly

IN THE DISTANCE I SAW A LARGE HERD OF BUFFALOES WHICH WERE
BEING CHASED AND FIRED AT BY TWENTY OR THIRTY INDIANS.

secreted him in the brush. Then I climbed up the steep side of the bank and cautiously looked over the summit; in the distance I saw a large herd of buffaloes which were being chased and fired at by twenty or thirty Indians. Occasionally a buffalo would drop out of the herd, but the Indians kept on until they had killed ten or fifteen. Then they turned back and began to cut up the game.

I saddled my horse and tied him to a small tree where I could reach him conveniently in case the Indians should discover me by finding my trail and following it. I then crawled carefully back to the summit of the bluff, and in a concealed position watched the Indians for two hours, during which time they were occupied in cutting up the buffaloes and packing the meat on their ponies. When they had finished this work they rode off in the direction whence they had come.

I waited till nightfall before resuming my journey, and then I bore off to the east for several miles, and by making a semicircle to avoid the Indians, I got back on my original course, and then pushed on rapidly to

Colonel Rice's camp, which I reached just at daylight.

Colonel Rice had been fighting Indians almost every day since he had been encamped at this point, and he was very anxious to notify General Terry of the fact. Of course I was requested to carry his dispatches. After remaining at Glendive a single day, I started back to find General Terry, and on the third day I overhauled him at the head of Deer Creek, while on his way to Colonel Rice's camp. He was not, however, going in the right direction, but bearing too far to the east, and so I informed him. He then asked me to guide the command, and I did so.

On arriving at Glendive I bade good-by to the General and his officers, and took pason the *Far West,* which was on her way down the Missouri. At Bismarck I left the steamer and proceeded to Rochester, New York, where I met my family.

THE LIFE
OF BUFFALO BILL

THE LIFE OF BUFFALO BILL

I

THE LITTLE BOY OF THE PRAIRIE

ONCE when Buffalo Bill was a tiny boy of seven or eight his father's family were camping on their way to Kansas. It happened that both his father and the guide were away from the little camp in search of food. It was at night and young Bill Cody was asleep. He was suddenly awakened by hearing a noise, and saw an Indian in the act of untying and leading away his own pet pony. The boy jumped up, grasped his rifle, and said,

"What are you doing with my horse?"

The Indian did not seem to be much disturbed at the little fellow's appearance, and said he would swap horses. Little Bill said he would not swap. The Indian only laughed at him. Then the boy held his gun

ready, and said again that he would not
swap; and in the end the big Indian, after
watching him keenly for a few minutes,
quietly mounted his old pony and rode away.
This is a good example of the nerve and
courage which have made him as a grown
man the best plainsman in our history.

Every boy, perhaps every man, loves to
read about the days of Indian fights, the
camping along the trails, the crossing of the
plains in prairie schooners, and the wild life
that belonged to what was once called the
Great American Desert—which now con-
tains thousands of farms and hundreds of
cities. It was a hard life; but it was so full
of real adventure, of actual danger, that it
had its own interest to those who lived it.
And although it is gone now forever, it will
always remain the most interesting part of
American history to the boys of our country.

That was the time when a man saved his
own life day by day, absolutely and solely
because he had greater courage or quicker
wit than his opponent, whether that opponent was an Indian, a stage robber, a flood,
a prairie fire, or any other form of danger.

THE LITTLE BOY OF THE PRAIRIE

To understand those days and the events and episodes as they occurred to the men who lived them, one must first get into one's mind the country they lived in and traveled over. It was a flat land stretching thousands of miles across the middle of the United States from the Missouri River to California, with here and there a huge range of mountains running north and south, guarded on either side by long lines of foothills. Sometimes there were stretches of forest; generally there was nothing but the flat plains covered with a rough wild grass. Between the Rocky Mountains and the Sierra Nevada there were the alkali plains, unfit for human habitation. All this country was inhabited by Indians who had been gradually driven westward from the Atlantic coast, who had been treated badly by white men, and who had become a fierce race of fighters and hunters. They considered the white man their natural prey. Whenever they saw a "pale face" it was fair and right in their minds to try to get his scalp; for hundreds of stories had been handed down from their fathers and grandfathers of the way in which the white man had killed their people and driven them from the land that had been theirs for centuries.

Over this country—a distance of two thousand miles—the buffaloes and the Indians roamed, and no white man had a home. There were no cities. There were practically no towns. The white man gradually moving west had got as far as the western counties of Arkansas, Missouri, and Iowa in 1850; the white men had settled the Pacific coast in California; there were no railroads; there was no way to communicate between the Missouri River and California, except on horseback or by driving huge wagons across these wild plains.

Any day, any moment, while the travelers were sitting in their great wagons, they might see some little specks coming toward them across the flat plain. Then came a scurrying to put the wagons in a circle with the horses and mules, men and women, in the center. In a moment a band of mounted Indians would rush down upon them; and unless they were ready these wild red men would ride through the train between the

wagons, frighten the mules and horses, separate one wagon from another, and after killing all the human beings, carry their goods
away. Sometimes it happened in the night.
Sometimes it happened in the day. And as
those who were not ready were always
killed, the result was that those who lived
and traveled across those plains were the
keenest and shrewdest of their kind—quicker
and shrewder than the Indians themselves.
Even if the Indians did not appear, it took
a good hunter to keep his little caravan sup-
plied with food. For the journey was a long
one; there were many breakdowns and delays; and in order to supply food for the
company the buffalo and deer of the plains
had to be hunted and killed.

That was the country and the people between 1850 and 1860. After the rush to
California for gold, it became evident that
there must be some regular system of communication between the outskirts of civilization in the East, and the outskirts of civilization in the West in California. It was just
at this time that the man who is known all
over the world as Buffalo Bill was born.

THE LIFE OF BUFFALO BILL

Buffalo Bill's father was named Isaac Cody. He lived on a farm in Scott County, Iowa, near a town named Le Clair, and there William Frederick Cody was born on the 26th of February, 1846.

When the California gold craze came in 1849, Isaac Cody, with thousands of other people, made up his mind to go across the plains to California and look for gold. But before he had much more than started he changed his mind and moved toward Kansas, where he hoped to find some place to settle on the frontier. Instead of taking his wife and children on such a dangerous expedition he left them with his brother, Elijah Cody, in Platt County, Missouri, and then started out in search of a new home. Finally, when young William was only seven or eight years old, his father settled near Fort Leavenworth, Kansas, and here the boy grew up in the midst of Indians and the wild life of the plains, and in the very thick of the early fights that occurred between the Northerners and Southerners over the question of slavery. It was a hard life and only those who were naturally fitted for it lived through it. Even at the age of seven or eight little Bill Cody naturally took to this sort of life. He loved adventure. He loved stories of Indians, scouts, and desperadoes, and he could fire a rifle pretty accurately almost as soon as he could carry one.

Finally the family settled in Salt Creek Valley in Kansas, which was on the line of one of the two trails, or roads—if they could be called roads—that stretched for two thousand miles or more across this waste of plain and mountain to California.

Day after day little Bill Cody would go out with his father, taking his rifle, to hunt, and he always had with him a famous dog named "Turk." The boy, and in fact all the children, loved Turk. He was as much one of the family as any of the children, and again and again gave warning of danger. There are many instances in which the dog practically saved the lives of at least one member of the family group. One day when Cody's two sisters were walking some distance from their home they heard a snarl, and looking up into a tree they saw a panther getting ready to spring upon them. Old

Turk, who was with them, was quite as well aware of the danger as they were; and while they hid in the bushes, he sat in front of them and grappled with the panther as it jumped to reach them. The whole incident took place in a moment, and before they realized what had happened, they saw their favorite dog in the act of being killed by the panther. Suddenly off in the distance they heard their brother Bill's familiar whistle calling his dog. Then on the instant, as they crouched there, expecting every moment to see the fight end with the death of the dog, a rifle shot rang out and the panther rolled over dead. That was a famous shot in itself for a boy of less than eight years, for both animals were rolling over and over in their fight, and it took not only nerve, but accurate aim, to hit the one and avoid the other.

The family had scarcely got settled in their new home when the father, who did not believe in slavery, got into discussions with other people of the county who had been brought up to hold slaves. Those were hard, dangerous men. They got angry quickly; they shot their pistols at one another without much provocation, and they feared neither death nor anything else because they were living in the midst of danger always. In one of these excited discussions as to whether slaves should be held in the new State of Kansas or not, Isaac Cody took a firm stand on his side, and was thereupon notified that if he did not leave the country he would be shot. He had to hide frequently in different parts of his own house at night when a body of men would come to kill him, and for days and days he lived in thickets near the house, his little son bringing him food every day.

Once when a party had come to the house in search of his father and had failed to find him, young Bill discovered that his pony was missing. He went out to look for it, and found that it had been stolen by a member of the lynching party named Sharp. He cried out to the man that that was his pony; whereupon the desperado laughed at him. Bill called him a coward and told him he would get even with him some day; and then suddenly getting an idea, he whistled for Turk, and set the dog on the man. The dog ran up to the pony and bit his hind legs, whereupon the little horse kicked vigorously and bucked until he had thrown Sharp off. Then began a hot discussion between Will and Sharp, the one setting the dog on, the other yelling to have him called off. But in the end Sharp was obliged to temporize. He returned the pony and went away as fast as he could run.

So the days went on until Isaac Cody was obliged to leave the country. One of the famous scout's first real adventures occurred at this time. The boy was scarcely ten years old when one night the family received information that their father was coming home to see them and to stay for one night, returning to Fort Leavenworth in the morning. In some way the men of the community discovered that he was coming. A party was sent out to capture him as he came through a wooded gulch, and the little family sat around the hearth, most of them in tears, with the certainty that their father would be killed that night.

Then the instinct of the young scout came

to the surface. Young Bill proposed that he should ride his pony to a place called Grasshopper Falls, where his father was staying, and warn him. The boy had been sick with a fever; but he got out of bed, mounted his pony, and started in the night to ride the thirty miles. He had only gone four or five when he heard a cry of, "Halt!" Instead of stopping, he leaned over Indian fashion behind his pony, so that nothing but one leg showed on the side from which the call came, and there he hung as the good horse rushed at his top speed through the ambuscade. As he did not stop, the men began firing at him, and he could hear the bullets flying over him. He got through safely, however, and succeeded in getting to Grasshopper Falls just as his father was starting. It is interest- to know that this ride taken in the night by a sick boy not old enough to go to school was ten miles longer than the famous ride of General Philip Sheridan in the Civil War.

Then came hard times for the little Cody family. The father died, and the mother had no means of supporting her children and keeping up the farm. Young Bill, then

THE LIFE OF BUFFALO BILL

eleven years old, made up his mind that it
was his duty to support them. He could not
stay at home, as he was not big enough to
attend to the work of the farm.

It seemed an almost impossible task, because in addition to all their poverty there
was a mortgage of one thousand dollars
against their farm, and if they did not pay
this shortly their own home would be taken
away from them. Mrs. Cody was a brave
woman, and she felt that if it were not for
that mortgage she could have managed to
scrape along and keep the family alive. In
the many talks which they had as to what
they should do, the boy told his mother that
if she could fight this claim he would try to
earn the money.

This was his idea. There was a firm—a
famous one in the history of that part of the
United States—named Russell, Majors &
Waddell, frontiersmen who had gradually
built up a line of freight wagons that went
from St. Joseph, Missouri, to San Francisco,
two thousand miles across the plains and
mountains, carrying the freight that was
shipped from the East to the West and

bringing back freight from California to the East. These goods were packed in huge wagons with big canvas tops, drawn by sometimes ten and sometimes twenty teams of oxen. There was so much danger in these trips from Indians and outlaws that they never started without several wagons in a little caravan, with a guard of frontiersmen all armed and ready to repel any attack from whatever source. Each night they camped in certain places along the trail where there was water and, if possible, wood. They cooked their own meals. They set up their pickets and guards, and started on again in the morning to the next camp. The journey took about a month; and time and time again the whole outfit would fail to appear at the other end. It had been attacked and all the men killed by Indians or by the robbers of the plains. And sometimes the next caravan would find the remnants of the wagons and the dead bodies of men and oxen. It was Bill Cody's idea to see if he could not get a chance to travel as what is called an "extra" on one of these caravans, and forthwith he presented himself at the office of the firm in

Fort Leavenworth. One of the members of the firm had known his father, and so he treated the boy kindly. But he told him frankly that a boy of his age would be of no use. Bill, however, said that he could ride and shoot, that he could herd cattle and do a lot of other things. He wanted to be an "extra." Finally, he was so earnest in his desire, that Mr. Majors consented; and there is an interesting document which was signed by the two which shows what was expected and what were the dangers of such work. This paper reads as follows:

"I, Wm. F. Cody, do hereby solemnly swear before the great and living God, that during my engagement with, and while I am in the employ of, Russell, Majors & Waddell, I will not, under any circumstances, use profane language, that I will not quarrel or fight with any other employé of the firm, and that in every respect I will conduct myself honestly, be faithful to my duties, and shall direct all my acts so as to win the confidence of my employers. So help me God."

And so the "boy extra" began his work. At night he slept in a blanket under a wagon, and by day he did whatever he was given to do.

Day after day, week after week, they traveled slowly over the huge plains, the "bull whackers"—the men who drove the huge oxen—constantly snapping their enormous whips and urging the beasts on as fast as possible. It was a monotonous life, except when some incident occurred, and then the incident was likely to be one of life and death, depending on the quickness, accuracy of aim, and alertness of the men in the "bull train." They had gone only about thirty-five miles from Fort Kearny, one of the places where they stopped near the Platte River, when young Bill suddenly saw the three pickets drop flat on the ground, and the next moment he heard shots and saw a band of Indians riding toward them. Instantly the men in the bull train—all frontiersmen—made a circle of the wagons, got into the circle themselves, and began firing at the Indians. The red men wheeled in a big curve, firing as they went, and then rode off a short distance on the plain out of gun shot and stood watching the white men.

THE LIFE OF BUFFALO BILL

Buffalo Bill has already told this story in his own words earlier in the book. But he does not tell what it seems impossible to believe—that this boy of eleven years saved the lives of the entire outfit; and so it is well to mention the fact here. The consultation which the men had while the Indians waited proved that it was useless to stay where they were. Indians began to come from all quarters and outnumbered the whites ten to one. It was therefore decided to leave the train to the mercy of the Indians and make a dash for a creek where they could hide behind the embankment. This was successfully carried out and they then started for Fort Kearny, walking in the water and keeping watch over the top of the bank. As night came on the little boy began to get tired and weak. He could not keep up with the others, and in the excitement and darkness they did not miss him as he gradually fell behind. So the little fellow was trudging along, his rifle over his shoulder, perhaps a hundred yards behind the party, when to his amazement he saw the feathered head of an Indian poke over the bank before him and behind the others of his party. The Indian did not see him, for he was looking toward the others. With the quickness and instinct which made Buffalo Bill what he was, the lad put up his rifle, and the first warning his friends had of any attack in the rear was the sound of a shot, and the sound, too, of the body of the dead Indian rolling down into the creek. That was Buffalo Bill's first Indian, and the story of the boy who had saved the bull train went all over the frontier country in an incredibly short space of time.

II

LITTLE BILL AT SCHOOL AND AT THE TRAPS

NOW began days of trouble for the young frontier boy. The family difficulties were not so serious as they had seemed at first. Mrs. Cody was able to keep the farm, and realizing that her boy, while promising to make a good frontiersman, was not getting any education, she showed him the necessity of having the "man of the family" go to school.

Near their home some of the settlers had contributed money for the building of a little schoolhouse and for the payment of a teacher who was to come from the East and teach their children. Mrs. Cody made up her mind that Bill should go there to school, and after much discussion he began his school days.

Those must have been strange school days as we think of school now. The little one-room shanty on the plain had nothing in it but a few boards of the simplest kind that would serve as desks, a stove, and a few, very few, books. The scholars were a wild lot, quite unused to any kind of discipline. There was no idea in their minds of promptness, of getting to school on time, of behaving while they were in school, or of studying very hard over their lessons. In fact, their parents had had very little education, and there was nothing in all that country that made people believe in any discipline. Then, too, the teacher was not a very good one. In fact, it would have been hard to get a man to go out on that wild frontier who could make a living in the East. So the school was a somewhat uproarious affair. The boys had numerous fights. They came when they liked. They went hunting or fishing as they saw fit. They got a good many beatings from the teacher and laughed over them afterward. They teased the girls, and again and again the school teacher, unable to cope with them, settled matters by driving them out of the little house and locking the door.

In the midst of this crowd of youngsters young Bill began his first day. He was known to them all and to all their parents for miles around as the boy who had saved the bull train, as a fine shot, and as a good deal of a hero. Besides this he was a terrible tease, not only to his own sisters, but to every one else's sisters.

Not many days had passed when a feud grew up between him and another boy of the school. This soon developed into fights, finally ending in the arrival of old Turk at the school. The school, like all other houses, had no cellar. It rested a foot or two above the ground. Bill's rival in the school was a boy named Gobel, and he, too, owned a dog. When Turk arrived in search of his young master the school was in session, and a moderate amount of order had been maintained for some time. Then suddenly the scholars and the teacher heard beneath them a fierce growl, then another, then a series of howls and cries. And everyone knew that within a few inches of them, only separated by the floor, there was a fine dogfight in progress. That was enough for the scholars. They jumped over their seats, crowded out through the door, and stood around the schoolhouse watching Turk and Gobel's dog fight. Each dog was urged on by one of the two factions. It was not long before Turk had beaten his rival and driven him away with his tail between his legs. Whereupon young Gobel said that although his dog might be beaten, he could lick Will Cody. That was enough for the young frontier boy, and, in spite of all the teacher could do, a ring was soon formed by the scholars and a thoroughbred prize fight started. Gobel was much larger and older than Will, and the latter knew that he would be beaten shortly. He must resort to some stratagem, and though it seems strange to us now, out on that frontier, and especially to a boy who had actually been obliged to kill men to save his own life, any means of winning the fight was right. So the little fellow thinking all the time while he was in the midst of his struggle, drew his knife and stuck it into the fleshy part of Steve Gobel's leg. The moment Steve saw the blood he screamed with terror and cried out that he was killed.

Thereupon all the children took to their heels and ran to tell their parents that Will Cody had killed Gobel. Then the teacher took a hand, and so did the parents of many of the children, and it looked as if it would go hard with poor Bill. At all events, he did not care to stay at home, and not knowing what else to do, he ran away down the trail, happening to come upon one of the wagon trains of his first employers, Russell, Majors & Waddell, as he ran. The boss of the outfit was a man named Willis, and when the boy told his story Willis promised to look after him and take him again as a boy extra, first offering to go back to the school with him and lick Gobel, and the teacher too, if Bill said so. It was only a few moments when Gobel's father and a couple of men came up to arrest the boy, but they had to deal with men who were used to that sort of thing every day of their lives, and the pursuers soon discovered that it was wise for them to turn around and go home. But there was no more school for young Cody at present, and so he again became a member of a bull train.

AT SCHOOL AND TRAPS

During this short term of service with the freighters the boy had another experience which nearly ended his career, and which to any boy who lives in a pleasant home and never sees any such life can scarcely be much more than a fairy tale, it is so terrible and seems so impossible. The boy had a short time with nothing to do between trips in the winter, and he decided, as money was necessary, to go on a hunting trip with a party of trappers. There was a chance of making considerable money by trapping animals and selling their furs. As a matter of fact, the trapping was very successful, and young Bill contributed distinctly his part to the family treasury. It was in the midst of this trip, while he was in an absolutely uninhabited country, making a round of his traps, that he came upon three Indians, each leading a pony loaded with skins. It was a case of three to one, and the moment he discovered them they discovered him. He saw the leading Indian put up his rifle and aim it at him. Here was a case, one of the many that came later, when the young frontier boy unquestionably saved his life by his own quickness and skill. Actually before the Indian, who was no greenhorn at such matters, could aim his rifle and fire, Will Cody had shot him dead. The other two Indians fired arrows, one of which went through the boy's hat; but without stopping, he turned around and cried, as if to his companions:

"Here they are! This way! This way!"

And then—all this taking place in an incredibly short space of time—he wounded one Indian with his revolver as the two turned and fled; so that, instead of being killed himself, he killed one Indian, wounded another, overcame the third, and marched into camp with their three ponies and all the skins that they had gathered.

It was on a similar trapping expedition that the following episode occurred. The boy had been so successful and had made so much money that he decided on another trip. Not finding any party of men starting out, he got up an expedition of his own with a friend of his named David Phillips. The two youngsters bought an ox-team wagon and started out. They were after beaver, and when they were somewhere in the vicinity of Fort Leavenworth they struck a country full of beaver dams. Here they camped in a cave in the hillside which they fixed up for a permanent home. They stored the food they had brought and went to work setting their traps. At every hour of the day and night they were likely to run upon Indians, who never waited to parley, but killed whatever white men they saw as soon as they came upon them, scalping them and leaving them dead or dying wherever they might have fallen.

These two boys, therefore, were constantly on the watch. Every bush, every tree, every rock, might conceal an Indian, and by practicing this instinct, just as a sailor on a ship will see a sail that anyone else might think was a cloud or a speck on the horizon, these boys of the plains could discover, in a range of many miles over plain or rolling country, the slightest thing that was unusual or unexplainable. A little spot of color in a tree or bush that was not exactly the color of a winter leaf would mean to them an ambuscade of Indians. The slightest impression in the earth which was different from impressions left there by nature meant the trail of a party of Indians. Every instant while they were moving along in the day or night their eyes were roaming over the country round about to pick out any one of these tiny but unusual signs.

The boys had been attending to their work of trapping for many days without seeing any unusual sign. One night they came to their camp and had eaten supper, when their oxen began to bellow and leap about. The boys grabbed their rifles, ran to the corral, and discovered that a bear was in the vicinity. Phillips fired first and wounded the animal. But that only made him the more savage. The boy just managed to leap out of the bear's way when Bill fired into his mouth and killed him. But it was a close call, as the dead beast fell actually on the body of Phillips. It was a case of having saved the boy's life, and the chance of returning the favor came only too soon.

It was the next day, when Bill Cody slipped and broke his leg. The other boy carried him back to the camp, made splints, bound up his leg, and stopped the bleeding; and then the two sat down to decide what should be done. The nearest settlement was a hundred miles away. It was absolutely impossible for Cody to walk that distance. His friend could not carry him, and in the fright which the bear had given the two oxen one had killed itself, and the other had become so maimed that it had to be shot. What the youngsters were to do they did not know. No one was nearer than a hundred miles, and there was no way of getting a boy with a broken leg that distance. Yet it was a case of starving to death or of doing something at once. Therefore the two trappers, hardly fourteen years old, decided that Phillips should start at once and walk the hundred miles for assistance.

To go and come back would take him twenty days at least. That meant twenty days lying in a cave for Bill, without his having the power even to get up and go outside. Yet there was nothing else to do, and the good nerve of the two boys was sufficient for the occasion.

Phillips made Cody as comfortable as he

could and put all the food they had near
him. They figured out just how much he
was to eat each day in order to hold out until assistance should be brought, and then
shaking hands, Phillips left him.

The poor boy felt too lonely and heart-
broken to eat much of anything in the first
day or two. He counted the days as they
passed by cutting a notch in a stick of wood
each day. Gradually his leg healed, and in
the course of two weeks he could move about
a little. That alone relieved the pressure of
loneliness, for hobbling to the mouth of the
cave and looking outside was a very different
thing from lying perfectly still in one position day after day. He tried to use up some
of the time by studying the school books
which his mother had asked him to take
with him, and it was in the midst of one of
these attempts to pass away the hours by
reading over again what he had already
read a dozen times, that he looked up and
saw an Indian in war paint standing inside
the cave gazing at him.

In a moment a dozen or more warriors
had followed the first. The boy thought his

HE LOOKED UP AND SAW INDIANS IN WAR PAINT STANDING
INSIDE THE CAVE, GAZING AT HIM.

last day had come, for the delay that had occurred already was a longer time than the Indians usually gave any white man to live if they were in a position to put him out of existence. The chief in his guttural tones, without changing his expression at all, said:

"How?"

Bill said: "How?" and then they looked at one another, the boy's mind flying along all the possible schemes which an expert frontiersman could think of to prolong a discussion that might possibly save his life. As he was thinking, gazing thus at the Indians one after another, he suddenly recognized one of them who was a chief named Rain-in-the-Face, an Indian whom he had once befriended in a way that the red man appreciates.

It seems that once, some time before, Bill had found the man in difficulty and had given him something to eat and a blanket to sleep in. Instantly the boy's mind, well aware of the peculiar kind of gratitude Indians feel, began to work upon this. First he showed his leg and the bandages and told the story of his mishap, gaining as much time as he could in that way. Then suddenly he turned to Rain-in-the-Face and reminded him of how once their positions had been exactly reversed and how he had helped the Indian to get what he most needed. Rain-in-the-Face remembered the episode perfectly, and after a consultation he told Cody that although he and his friends were out in search of scalps, they would not molest him, but that that was the limit of their kindness.

The Indians ransacked the cave, took everything that was of value from it, leaving only a small amount of food. And yet after they were gone the boy was so thankful for the chance that had thrown this one Indian in his way and had saved his life that he could not even complain of the starvation which stared him in the face. He took what little food was left and divided it up, allowing ten days beyond the twenty for the return of Phillips, and kept strictly to the portion each day that would keep him in some sort of food until the thirty days were up.

A day or two after the episode of the Indians a heavy snowstorm set in, and lasted for so long that when it finally ceased the mouth of the cave was entirely covered with snow. That seemed almost the last straw, for little or no light came into the cave, the cold was intense, and the boy was unable to go out. Hour by hour, day in and day out, he sat there, unable to read any more and without any appetite for the little food he could allow himself.

Three weeks passed—one day over the time in which Phillips might have returned. The little fellow's mind almost gave way from the strain that was put on him as he sat there with night following day, and no change—only expectancy.

Twenty-eight days passed. He had but a day or so more of food. If help did not come within the next three days at the most, he would starve to death. To add to his misery, most of the wood that had been left was used up.

So the boy sat on the twenty-ninth day, huddled over the little flame that he could spare himself, hardly realizing now the passage of time, when he suddenly heard his name called. It seemed to him that he must be dreaming. He sat perfectly still listening, unable even to make a reply, and then the name rang out again and was repeated time after time. With all the strength he had left he answered the call, and it was his answering cry that enabled Phillips and the relief party to find the cave and begin digging through the snow.

When the two boys came together Bill Cody's nerves gave way and he was carried out more dead than alive. But he was alive and bound to have many more of these hairbreadth escapes that make perhaps as extraordinary a record as could be told of any man who has ever lived.

These adventures, which read to-day as if they came out of a wild, unreal story of adventure, happening as they did in the life of this boy not yet fifteen years old, prepared the way for a youth and early manhood of such extraordinary usefulness to the plains that Cody by the time the Civil War came was one of the most expert frontiersmen, guides, and scouts that existed in the United

States. And yet in 1860 he was but fifteen years old, too young, in other words, to go to college to-day, younger than most boys now when they get their first shotgun or rifle.

III

The Pony Express Rider

AT the time when the Civil War broke out Cody was too young to enlist. No regiment would take him, and besides, his mother, who was in feeble health and who had all the family to look out for, begged and prayed him to stay at home, as she said it was more important for him, the man of the family, to watch over them than to put his services at his country's disposal. The boy wanted to go. It was a natural contingency for a young man brought up as he had been brought up. Yet he gave up his ambition for his mother. Bill promised his mother that he would never go to war as long as she was alive, but that as he must do something to earn money, he had to go to work at once. His chance came with an opportunity to join a group of men who will be read about as long as there is any history of the United States. Their work only lasted a few years, but it was so extraordinary, so exciting, so near to the ideal of a life of adventure, that it stands out more important than many an era in this country's history which had greater results and extended over a longer time.

The firm of Russell, Majors & Waddell, who have already been mentioned, increased in importance because they were the only men who carried out on a large scale successfully the business of transporting freight across the desert and the mountains to California. But as California grew—and it grew very fast in a few years—there came a demand for a speedier method of communication between the Western frontier in the East and the Eastern frontier in the West. Those two thousand miles of waste land consumed a month or more when transportation was by means of bull trains. It did not matter very much with freight, but in the transportation of money, of letters, of business arrangements that time grew to be too long for advancing civilization.

The great freight transporters, therefore,

conceived the idea of getting up a scheme for carrying a few letters at a much faster rate from St. Joseph to San Francisco by means of a single horseman riding a pony at full speed. Their idea was that a man should mount a swift pony, well tried for his endurance before starting; that this man should ride fifteen miles straight out into the desert, and that at the end of the fifteen miles there should be a station, a house with a couple of men in it, who would have another pony ready. The horseman was to ride up to this shanty, jump to the ground with his bag of letters, immediately jump on the fresh pony, and rush along another fifteen miles to a similar station. Some of these stations were in settlements, some were in towns, but most of them were on the bleak prairies or in the hills of the Rocky Mountains. The trail was the same as that used by the freight bull trains. The bull-train stations were of course used, but it was necessary to increase the number of stations. Some of the divisions were longer than others. But the average was a distance of forty-five miles; that is, the man who rode one of these divisions of the two thousand miles, rode fifteen miles on one pony, fifteen miles on the second, and fifteen miles on the third. Then he began his return trip of forty-five miles. The longest division was two hundred and fifty miles.

Sometimes the country was open and moderately easy for riding. Sometimes it was up rocky gulches or through forests where the riding was hard. It required in the men the hardest kind of physique and endurance, in the ponies surefootedness as well as swiftness. Sometimes in order to keep up the schedule the men were obliged to cover twenty-five miles in an hour on flat country, in order to make up for slower going in the hills. They received about one hundred and twenty-five dollars a month, which was very high pay. But that gave the promoters of the scheme their choice among the best men of the frontier.

The letters were carried in mail pouches or bags that hung over the saddle, and no rider was allowed to carry more than twenty pounds. In order to get as much mail within the twenty pounds as possible letters were written on tissue paper. Whatever money was carried was in paper, and one Eastern newspaper printed a special edition on tissue paper for use only on this famous Pony Express. So in the twenty pounds there were hundreds of letters. In fact, the paper was so thin that even a hundred letters would not occupy a space larger than that occupied by an ordinary monthly magazine to-day. The mail pouches were waterproof, and once locked at St. Joseph, Missouri, they were not opened until they were delivered in Sacramento, California, two thousand miles away.

It seems almost incredible, but that distance was covered in a time that was extraordinarily short for those days, when one remembers that the whole journey was made by running ponies. It was an exciting time when the first pony was ready and saddled at the offices of Russell, Majors & Waddell, in St. Joseph. A large crowd gathered long before the appointed time for starting, and when the pony was brought forth he was greeted with cheers. At the exact moment a frontiersman came out of the office, threw the pouch over the saddle, leaped on the pony, and started off at the top speed the pony was capable of, followed by the cries and cheers of the crowd. This first trip was started on the 3d of April, 1860. That journey, where the mail bags were thrown across the ponies and carried by a number of riders, took ten days to do the two thousand miles. It was an average of two hundred miles a day, or between eight and nine miles an hour for every hour of the twenty-four for ten days, including all stops and all delays. But in a short time the average trip was made regularly in nine days, and the fastest trip was made when President Lincoln's inaugural address was carried over the two thousand miles in seven days and seventeen hours.

When Cody was looking for work he conceived the idea of enlisting as one of the Pony Express riders, and he went to the office of the company and asked if he could not be one of the riders. They told him that he was too young, as he was then only a little over fourteen. But he insisted he could do it, and finally they gave him the shortest trip, a ride of thirty-five miles with three changes of ponies.

When the time came for him to be ready for the first trip the boy was outside of his station with his pony ready, looking across the prairie for the rider who was to bring the mail pouches from the next station. Close upon time the man appeared. Drawing up to the station he jumped off, threw the bag to Cody, who in turn leaped into his saddle with it and started on his fifteen miles. He reached his first station on time, dismounted, and mounted a fresh pony which was standing ready, and started on the second relay. And so with the third, until he finished his thirty-five miles and threw the bag to the next man, who was waiting. And within an hour he was ready again for the rider coming from the direction of San Francisco. As soon as he had the mail he mounted a fresh pony and rode back over the same thirty-five miles.

Thus the boy did seventy miles every day for three months. But endurance was not the only quality the rider must have. Through most of the whole route there was constant danger of a "hold up" either from Indians or from outlaws, who knew that the bag frequently contained money. He must be as alert and as good a frontiersman in the knowledge of Indian warfare as he was a good horseman. It was some time before the boy had any incident other than the ordinary episodes of the long ride. However, the time came.

He was riding as fast as his pony could go through a ravine one day when there sprang out in front of him in the narrow track a man with his rifle at his shoulder. Young Cody knew enough to know that the man had what was called the "drop" on him. There was nothing to do but pull up and await events. It was a white man—a desperado of the plains. He told the boy that he meant him no harm, but that he wanted the money in the bag. Cody could do nothing but sit quietly on his pony. But always alert, always on the watch for every opportunity, in a situation that, young as he was, he had been in many times before, he kept a keen eye on the man while appearing to submit. The outlaw was careless enough to approach the pony from the front, and as he got within reach the young horseman by a trick that he had used many times before made the pony rear so suddenly that his fore foot struck the man in the head and knocked him senseless.

Bill knew that somewhere in the vicinity the highwayman had a horse. He at once dismounted, bound the man hand and foot while he was insensible, and then began to hunt for the horse in the bushes. He found him a few rods away, and when he got back his opponent had come to. Unbinding his legs, Bill forced him to mount his own horse, and then strapped him on. Although the young Pony Expressman was late at the next station, the fact that he had brought in a robber and had saved his mail pouch was quite sufficient excuse for the delay of the mail that day.

At the end of a few months the work proved too severe for him to continue, and he was laid off as supernumerary—that is, a man who could be called on to ride in any emergency. It was not long, however, before he made application for another job on the Pony Express. He went to Fort Laramie and looked up a man named Slade, who was agent of the line there. Slade told him he was too young, but on hearing his name he slapped him on the shoulder and said that he had heard of him before and that he would give him a job. This run was from Red Buttes to a place called Three Crossings, and the distance was seventy-six miles. The boy started running this route regularly each day, and for a time had no unusual experience. One day, however, having made the run out of seventy-six miles, he found, when he arrived at his last station, that the man who was supposed to carry the bag to the next station, a distance of eighty-five miles, had been wounded by Indians. Bill offered to go on and carry the bag over that man's section, and as there was no one else to do it he was sent on. This second division covered a distance of one hundred and sixty-one miles. That made one continuous route of three hundred and twenty-two miles out and back without stopping. In that time he rode twenty-one ponies and made the longest trip ever made by a Pony Express rider.

It was while on this route that one day he suddenly came upon a man who appeared from behind a large rock as Cody passed. There was no time for thought, and Bill immediately reached for his revolver, but upon seeing him the man dropped his rifle and came forward. He turned out to be a famous character of the plains named "California Joe," and on seeing the young boy he immediately asked him if he were not Bill Cody. Then the frontiersman told him that a little way back on the road he had what he called "a little misunderstandin' with two men, and now I has to plant 'em."

It was only a little later that, as Bill left one of the stations, the boss called to him to look out, there were reports of Indians in the vicinity. Cody said he would, and started away at breakneck pace. Here again, as many times before and after, the boy's instinctive knowledge and immediate perception of anything, no matter how small, that was unusual or unnatural on the plains saved his life. Always keeping a keen watch, he suddenly saw above the top of a pile of rocks something that he knew was not put there by nature. It was a little speck of color, and long before any average human being would have seen it at all he knew that it was a feather in the headdress of an Indian in war paint. He did not stop or turn. He kept on at his furious pace until he was within rifle shot. Then ducking behind his pony, he turned him instantly off the trail, and at the same moment a puff of smoke from behind the rock showed that his guess had been true. The bullet went where the rider should have been, but it missed by the swerve which he had caused the pony to make. Out sprang two warriors, and a party of Indians appeared from a little distance further away. And now it became a ride for life. As he approached the end of the valley, which narrowed into a point, he saw that some of the Indians on the slopes were riding down to cut off his track. He watched his opportunity, and luckily for him those Indians had no rifles. He saw them fit the arrows to their bows, waited for the right moment, and just before the leading Indian fired his arrow the boy shot him with his revolver. When he reached the next station

he found that his pony had two arrows sticking in its flesh.

At this time the Pony Express had to be
stopped for some time on account of the
number of Indians who were lying in wait
all along the trails to capture the riders, and
so the boy was once more out of a job.

He became a supernumerary again, and
as there were days in which he had nothing
to do, he was in the habit of going out hunting, selling the skins of the animals he shot.
On one of these trips he came upon a group
of horses tied near a stream, and hearing
voices in a dugout cave near by, he went to
investigate. It turned out that the men were
a group of prairie ruffians. They supposed
him to be an advance scout in search of
themselves, and for a few moments there was
a quick play of wit against wit.

They asked him where he came from. He
pointed backward. They asked where his
horse was. He said it was down by the
stream. They asked him to go and get it and
join them. He said he would, volunteering,
with the keenness of men whose lives are
always at stake, to leave his gun with them.

THE PONY EXPRESS RIDER

That allayed suspicion for the moment, but they even went so far as to send two of their number with him. The boy, as they reached the horse, carelessly said that he had shot some game and would pick it up, in the meantime asking the men to lead his horse on ahead. Then turning behind the second man, he struck him a blow with his revolver and shot the other. Mounting his pony, Cody then dashed down the ravine. In a moment the whole party were after him. It was certain that he would soon be overtaken, as his own pony was tired and theirs were fresh. Bill turned the corner of some rocks and, dismounting, gave the pony a slap and sent him tearing down the ravine, while he himself hid in the bushes and watched the whole party tear by in the pursuit of the riderless horse. He then calmly walked back to the station at Horseshoe and told of the adventure. Such experiences as this followed one after another, until in 1863, with the Civil War in full progress, Cody, then seventeen years old, received word that his mother was dying. He went immediately to their home, and arrived in time to see his mother before she died.

It was a sad household that gathered together after the burial, and when the children talked over what they should do, they were astonished to hear that Cody had made up his mind to enlist at once in the Northern army. He had kept his word with his mother and had not become a soldier as long as she lived; but now that she was dead and the family homestead out of debt, he was free from all promises.

He at once enlisted, and his regiment was soon ordered to the front, but the young man was so able as a scout that he soon came to be used on special duty. Then, too, his fame as a plainsman was well known, and it reached military headquarters long before he himself arrived. He was at once selected, therefore, as a bearer of military dispatches at Fort Larned, and one of his first escapades took place soon after he was put upon this work. Some of the Southerners bore a grudge against him that dated back to the time when he had saved his father from them. These men—now on the Southern side—

heard of his journey and laid in ambush by a stream in a gulch where it was necessary for him to cross on account of the ford. They hid their horses in a clump of trees and went to a cabin near the ford to wait for his arrival. Darkness came on before he reached the spot, and as by this time the young man had acquired the habit of absolutely observing everything at all times about him, he soon discovered the fresh tracks of horses. Without any other object than the natural instinct to find the reason for everything that presented itself, he quietly dismounted, followed the trail, and found the five horses. It was evident that there were five men near by watching for him.

The only thing to do was to ride on as quietly as possible and try to make the ford. He was in the act of entering the water when he heard their cries, and, urging his horse into the stream, he turned in his saddle, and before any of the five could pull a trigger he had shot one of them. Still he spurred the horse on, turned again and shot another. But the others were firing now, and so Cody fell forward across his horse and was lucky enough to make the other side of the stream. There he was safe, because the other three were not mounted.

When the scout returned with answers to the dispatches he became very wary as he approached the ford. There were no signs, however, of an attacking party, and, coming up to the shanty, he found one of the men whom he had shot dying there alone. The man had been left by his pals with enough food to last him until he should die, and Bill discovered that he was a man whom he had known from his earliest boyhood, and who had been a supposed friend of his father. As the man was near his end, the boy gave him water and sat by him until he died. He then returned to Fort Larned.

IV

"Bill Cody, the Scout"

WITH his entrance into the United States army "Bill Cody," as he had come to be known, arrived at man's estate, although he was scarcely eighteen years of age. He was known not only all over the West, but every army headquarters knew of the skillful frontiersman, and even at that early date most boys of the United States had read some part of his life in the newspapers.

Now his work became that of a man, and he had plenty of narrow escapes during the war, which in their way were as remarkable as his experiences on the plains. For example, once General Smith, who was in charge of headquarters at Memphis, got hold of him and told him that he wished to get some information and have some maps drawn of the position of the Confederate troops; and that it was impossible to secure this unless he could find a man who would go into the Confederate camp in disguise. Cody immediately consented to go. It did not seem any more dangerous or any less honorable than carrying out the regular life of a scout and Indian hunter of the plains.

Just before the trip he had captured a man whom he knew, but who sided with the Southerners—a man named Nat Golden, who had been one of Russell, Majors & Waddell's freightmen. On this man he found some dispatches, which he promptly read. Golden was such an old friend that Cody took the papers from him, and when the man was arrested, nothing being found on him to make him a spy, he was simply imprisoned. Bill never told. With these papers in his possession and dressed in the Confederate uniform, the spy entered the Confederate lines, after telling General Smith what was in the dispatches.

He was, of course, immediately halted by the pickets, to whom he stated that he was a Confederate soldier with information for the general. After being disarmed he was taken to General Forrest, and a conversation then took place in which Cody told Forest that Golden had been captured, and that as he was being taken prisoner he had handed Cody the dispatches, asking him to take them to General Forrest. The story seemed so plausible that the General allowed him to stay in camp. And for two days he kept his eyes open, drew plans, and was ready to leave, when he came near losing his presence of mind, as well as his life, by discovering General Forrest talking with Golden himself, who had escaped from the Union lines. He knew that there was no time for delay. Golden, having no idea that Cody was in the Confederate lines, would tell Forrest the whole story as it actually happened, and the General would at once have him arrested. He went, therefore, apparently in great calmness, to his tent, got his horse saddled, and rode quietly toward the picket line. No one suspected that anything was the matter. No one paid any attention to him. As he got to the picket the sergeant spoke to him, recognized him, and allowed him to pass.

He was outside the lines—in fact, he was between the Union and the Confederate lines —when he heard the sound of a squad of cavalry approaching. Then he put his horse to the run and in a moment discovered that a troop of Confederate cavalry was approaching from behind to meet a troop of Union cavalry approaching from the front. The one thought a spy was escaping; the other thought that a deserter or a spy was approaching. It was a hard situation. Fortunately, he got into some timber, and as he came out on the other side he discovered the Union lines. But it was not safe for him to approach in Confederate uniform, and so, with the knowledge that the Confederate cavalry was looking for him in the woods, Cody calmly dismounted at the spot where he had left his uniform, changed his clothes, and was able to lay his maps and report before General Smith within forty-eight hours from the time he had left.

After some further experiences with the force at the front, Cody was assigned to duty at St. Louis. Office work palled on him, however, and he soon procured his release, as the war was practically over. He then returned to Fort Leavenworth and looked again for a job. This time it turned out to be the work of driving the famous overland stage which ran from St. Joseph to Sacramento, doing the two thousand miles in nineteen days on the average. This stage was another of the enterprises of the great firm of Russell, Majors & Waddell. It was a difficult enterprise, too. The stage frequently carried large sums of money, and was therefore frequently held up by desperadoes or Indians.

No one seemed very anxious to undertake the work of driver, although it was well paid. And the now famous Indian scout saw his opportunity again of making relatively large sums of money by taking risks that few others would take. He was at once offered the opportunity on his application, and started driving the coach for what was called a division—that is, two hundred and fifty miles.

Those were strange old coaches. One of them may be seen to-day by any boy who will go to Buffalo Bill's famous Wild West

Show and watch the old Deadwood coach drive around the ring. They were large-wheeled wagons swung on braces. They had to be strong, for they went over the most frightful roads one can imagine. Passengers could ride inside or on top, and every one who traveled went as fully armed as he could. There never was a time in the night or day when the coach was not apt to be attacked. And if it were attacked, the man on the box was the first one shot. Cody's run was from Fort Kearny to Plum Creek, and he drove six horses. When he took hold of the job he was warned that Indians were all about, and rumors came thicker and thicker in the first month of his driving.

Nothing happened, however, with the exception of one trip, where he saved the coach and the lives of all in it by a daring rush through a stream in the face of a party of Indians. But shortly after this he was told by the division superintendent, as he left Fort Kearny, that in the coach was a very large amount of money being sent in a box to Plum Creek. It was a question whether the existence of this treasure had become known or not. At any rate, Cody said he would be on the watch. First, before mounting on the box, he looked over the passengers—and here again was the same habit of looking at everything and everybody that might have any relation to the situation. He did not like the looks of two of the passengers, and as the conductor, who always traveled with the driver on the trip, was suddenly prevented from going, his suspicions became keener.

Again the keen boy decided that the thing to do was to take time by the forelock. He had proceeded only a part of the distance after all but the two passengers had left when he pulled up the coach and got down as if to examine the running gear. Then he asked the two men to help him. As they started to come out of the coach Cody pointed two revolvers at them and held them up in the most approved fashion. He made them throw out their revolvers, then bound them and put them back in the coach.

Something that one of the men had said made him think that they were part of a gang, the other members of which were somewhere in ambush along the trail. On reaching the first relay station he deposited his prisoners with the agent and then started on.

There were no other passengers. He had no sooner gotten away from the station than, stopping again, he cut open one of the cushions of the coach, and taking the money from the box, put it inside the cushions and then patched up the opening. After that he remounted the box and rode on.

Within an hour, while driving through a bit of timber, the expected happened. The coach was held up by half a dozen men. They started to look for the treasure. Cody told them a long story of two men who had been riding as passengers, who had held him up in a lonely spot, taken the treasure, and disappeared into the timber. The gang immediately recognized their confederates, and in a fury at being thus deceived, they waited only long enough to ask him if they were mounted. On receiving an answer that they were not and also a description of the direction they had taken, the highwaymen left him in peace and rode in hot haste after their confederates.

And the driver of the overland stage finished his journey and deposited the treasure into the hands that it was intended for.

V

The Indian Campaigns with the Army

ANYONE who will read the history of the United States after the Civil War will come upon a long series of campaigns of the United States army in the West against the American Indians. These Indians, as has already been said, constantly being more and more confined, had now only the great American desert and the Rocky Mountains to live upon. They existed there in enormous numbers. They hunted the almost limitless herds of buffalo and deer. They fought, whenever opportunity offered, whatever white men came upon them. The attempt of the government was to give the Indians certain territories on which they could live in different parts of that country. These territories were called Indian reservations, and some of them still exist; but at that time—that is, between 1870 and 1880—

the Indians were still in their native wild civilization, and declined to be limited to these reservations.

They had no desire to become farmers. They wanted to roam over the plains, and hunt, and fish, and live as they were born to live. They could not be made like white men. And hence the result was a series of campaigns which gradually exterminated most of them and killed the spirit of the others. One of these campaigns was the famous fight of General Custer, whose command was practically annihilated in the famous battle of Little Big Horn. Here again the qualities of Cody came into great demand. He was one of the greatest scouts in these Indian campaigns. His experiences, his fights, would number into the hundreds in a short decade. General Sheridan, who was put in command of the troops to quell the Indian uprising, made him the chief of his scouts, and during these years he was constantly at work leading the American troops against the Indians.

Some time before he had acquired the name which now every boy in this country and almost every boy in the civilized world knows him by—"Buffalo Bill"—and the story of how this name was given to him is well worth the telling.

Cody had always been a great shot—not only an accurate, but a wonderfully quick shooter. This skill and quickness had saved his life many times. When he was not at work at some specific duty he would hunt buffaloes, riding forth over the plains on a horse he had trained to hunt. As a herd of buffaloes—and there were hundreds of them —was seen approaching some camp where Cody was, he would mount his horse, throw the reins on his neck, and sit quietly while the animal ran diagonally toward the herd at full speed, selected of his own will the last of the herd, and worked with all his keen, nervous ability until he brought his rider close alongside the shaggy animal. There is but one spot that is very vulnerable in a buffalo. You may shoot a dozen times and hardly wound him, but if one shot reaches the vital spot, the animal drops dead in his tracks. Again and again the men of the plains have seen Cody start out on his horse and within a few minutes from the firing of the first shot drop ten or a dozen of the wild beasts of the prairie.

The story of how the name of Buffalo Bill came to be given to him by common consent is this: There was a man named William Comstock who had been called by his friends "Buffalo Bill" because he was such a successful buffalo hunter. When he heard that Cody was being called "Buffalo Bill" too, he disputed his right to that title. Cody heard of it, and told some of the officers of the army post that if there was any dispute, he for one was willing to settle it by an actual contest in buffalo killing. Comstock was as game as Cody, and accepted the challenge. And so the plainsmen arranged the contest.

They settled upon a huge tract of prairie near Sheridan, Kansas, and when the appointed day arrived everybody who could reach the spot came to witness the contest. Officers, soldiers, railroadmen, scouts, pioneers, and all the inhabitants of that country gathered in a large crowd. Judges were appointed and the two claimants to the title were on hand. It was an easy matter in those

days and in that place to find a herd of
buffaloes, so that within an hour after the
start they had sighted a herd and started for
the hunt.

As soon as the herd was sighted the two
men separated, each working on his own account and getting all the buffaloes he could.
Cody killed thirty-eight, to twenty-three for
Comstock, and the sight of sixty-one buffaloes lying dead upon the plain must have
been a wonderful one.

Then they had a gala lunch, and in the
afternoon started again. And then the final
crowning feat was apparent. In the second
contest Cody, in order to leave no doubt of
the matter, rode his horse without either saddle or bridle, and even then he killed
eighteen to the other's fourteen. From that
time on to this day no one has questioned his
right to the title of "Buffalo Bill."

It would be impossible here to go into the
many episodes that occurred while Bill,
under the title of Colonel William F. Cody,
was chief of the United States Army Scouts.
It is only possible to say that in that capacity
he not only made it possible for the United

States army to accomplish a work impossible without scouts who had been brought up in that kind of fight, but it is safe to say that if General Custer had had him with him, the frightful massacre of Little Big Horn would never have occurred. But in all that time Buffalo Bill was at work upon his chosen profession, with the exception of a short time when, against his will, he was made a justice of the peace.

There is an interesting and amusing episode told of his short legal career that is worth mentioning briefly here. Shortly after his appointment, which was made because of the necessity of having a justice of the peace at hand in the army post, a couple came to him to be married. He was very much disturbed and embarrassed, scarcely knowing what to do, but he got along all right until the end of the service, and then, to the amazement of the assembled party, he ended all by saying:

"Whom God and Buffalo Bill hath joined together, let no man put asunder."

In the midst of these years of scouting in the Indian fights the great Western scout was always in difficulty as to the management of his financial affairs. He always has said that he was not born a business man. When he had money he spent it like a gentleman, no matter how much it was. Once when he was not busy in Indian campaigning he conceived the idea of representing on the stage certain phases of life on the plains in order to make some money. The first venture took place in Rochester, New York. In order to make the show as realistic as possible, he himself and two other scouts were put into a play written especially for them, and the descriptions of the first performance make an episode in Buffalo Bill's life that must have been as amusing and as extraordinary as the episodes of his life on the plains were exciting and dangerous. The three were stagestruck from the time the curtain went up, and all of them forgot their lines. But Buffalo Bill, finding that nothing was going to happen and realizing that the audience were sitting in their seats expecting something to happen, answered the questions put to him by the manager and told a story. That poor manager must have had a bad quarter of an hour. He was also taking part in the piece, and was utterly at a loss what to say or do. Bill told a story of one of his experiences on the plains in his own language. This proving to meet with the approval of the audience, the manager continued asking questions, drawing forth story after story, so that when the play ended the audience felt full of enthusiasm for the extraordinary show, which in reality did not contain one single line of the original drama.

The scheme was not successful, however, and some years later Buffalo Bill got together some friendly Indian chiefs and some frontiersmen and constructed a simple play of the plains which was an immense success. At different times for five years this play— "The Scout of the Plains"—was played in nearly every city of any size in the United States. Frequently it would be having a run in some town when word would come from a commanding officer at a Western army post that the Indians were on the warpath again. Then the play would be closed, and the scouts, with their chief at their head, would hasten to the plains and begin again their real warfare, returning to the sham fights of the play when the real ones were over.

And it was this remarkable success in representing to people in Eastern cities the actual life on the plains that gave Colonel Cody the courage to carry out an idea which had been in his mind for many years—that is, of putting before people a true representation of the different phases of the life in that immense country, thousands of miles in length and width, which existed between 1840 and 1870, and which has now gone forever.

VI

Buffalo Bill and His Show

THERE is only a word to be said of Buffalo Bill's "Wild West," because the space at our command does not make it possible to tell the whole story in detail. The enterprise is now one of huge proportions, but it started much smaller. The reason for its enormous popularity and increase is that it is almost unique among plays or shows of every kind. For it gives to the audience a real picture, with real characters, of a most exciting period of civilization in this country that never has existed anywhere else, and that never will exist again. The Indians that have mock fights in Buffalo Bill's arena to-day are absolutely the same men who used to track him and try to kill him in the Indian campaigns twenty or thirty years ago. The Deadwood coach that is attacked in the arena by Indians with the shooting of guns is the same coach that used to run across the plains and that has time and time again been attacked in the same way, but with very different intent. The cowboys and frontiersmen who ride are the same men who used to live on the plains and herd cattle, and the ponies they ride are the bucking bronchos of the West.

There have often been doubts expressed as to the reality of some of this. One instance is enough to show the contrary. When the great Wild West Show went to Europe and traveled about in the ancient cities of Italy, they came finally to Rome and gave their daily exhibition there. In one of the boxes sat an Italian nobleman, the Prince of Sermonetta, who made the statement to his friends that he doubted whether the broncho busters—the men who ride the bucking bronchos—were really as good riders as they seemed. He thought the ponies were trained to buck.

This came to the ears of Buffalo Bill, and he answered it in his usual polite but sturdy fashion. Then the nobleman met him and told him that he had some wild horses on his estate in the country that had never been ridden and could not be controlled except in a mass. Buffalo Bill at once said that if he would have the horses brought to his arena some afternoon during the show he would like to have his men make a try at riding them. Nothing pleased the nobleman more, and of course the experiment was advertised all over Italy.

On the appointed day the horses were brought on in cars. There was considerable difficulty and a good deal of excitement in getting them out of the cars and into the arena. As soon as they found themselves loose after being cooped up in such undignified fashion, they were wild indeed. The arena was cleared of everything except those furious beasts, and then half a dozen cowboys calmly walked in with their lariats to make the trial. It was probably the most interesting exhibition ever given by the Wild West Show. Quietly and warily the cow punchers threw their lassoes, wound them about the feet of the horses, threw them, and held them down. Then they saddled and bridled them, and then the riding began. The show was not materially delayed; the audience left and got home at the usual time; but before they had quitted the arena every one of the wild horses was ridden quietly and in dignified fashion around the ring and up in front of the nobleman's box, and it was reported that no one was more pleased than that same nobleman himself.

There are many additional and interesting features to Buffalo Bill's show to-day, such as the Cossack riders, the San Juan battle, and the regiments of different European armies. But they do not add to the value of what will go down in history as "Buffalo Bill's Wild West." That is all true as gold. That is justly remarkable because of the real way in which it tells a real story, and if the boy of to-day who reads this would like to see what the Indians and the white men of the Western plains were in those days, how they fought, how they traveled, and how they lived, he may see it still by going to see the show. He will never see it anywhere else again.

In ending this little sketch of a remarkable man it is worth telling an episode of the experience of these natives of the wilderness in the midst of the centuries-old cities of the Old World. Everywhere the company went in England, in Europe, the famous scout was entertained by royalty and entertained them in return. One day after they had opened in London the King, then the Prince of Wales, expressed a desire to see the show. A box was prepared and the royal party attended. The whole exhibition was so new and interesting that in a short time the Prince went again, and expressed a desire to ride around the ring in the Deadwood coach. Buffalo Bill was ready and called for five passengers. The five passengers who accepted were the Prince of Wales himself on the box beside Buffalo Bill, and four kings who happened to be visiting in England—the King of Denmark, the King of Saxony, the King of Greece, and the Crown Prince of Austria. As usual, the coach started. But this time the Indians who attacked and the cowboys who rescued the coach had been instructed to "do something a little extra," to give a little louder yells, to fire a few more shots. And it is no wonder if, as the rumor goes—though proof does not exist—that before the ride was over some of the four kings were under the seats. When the trip was finished and the Prince of Wales congratulated Buffalo Bill, he said to him:

"Colonel, did you ever hold four kings like that before?"

And Cody replied: "I have held four kings more than once. But, your Royal Highness, I never held four kings and a royal joker before."

THE END